Dr. Marc Gafni & Dr. Kristina Kincaid

THE 12 FACES OF EROS

Selections from

a return to eros

The radical experience of being fully alive

Paintings & drawings by Kohlene Hendrickson

THE 12 FACES OF EROS

Contents 3

To… Sally Kempton,
Louise Smith,
Margaret Kincaid,
Karla Kincaid and
Tracy Woodward

awakening

Preface

The Future of Love, Sex, and Eros

toward a post-tragic sexual politics of eros

There are three primary levels of consciousness through whose prism we experience our lives. We will call these three levels the pre-tragic, tragic, and post-tragic.

Pre-tragic is the stage before tragedy. Life is good. Life is delightful. Life makes sense. It is ordered and reasonable. During the pre-tragic state we also experience pain and suffering, but our pain and suffering are not tragic. We are able to explain to ourselves and our intimates what hap- pened. We might use religious, psychological, or scientific explanations. Explanation saves our suffering from being tragic.

The second level of consciousness is the tragic. The goodness of life is broken up by suffering, but we no longer feel able to explain it. The rules break down. Perhaps the suffering is more intense than any we have experienced before. Alternatively, our trust in the religions or philosophies of life that undergirded our explanations have been shaken, often irrevocably. Our lives feel empty and meaningless, "a tale told by an idiot, full of sound and fury, signifying nothing."We are overwhelmed by the tragic nature of life itself. We may continue to function, love, and even be highly effective achievers. But our joy mechanism is broken. We are cut off from the natural joy we once felt from the essential goodness and primal aliveness of life.

Most people live their lives at either level one or level two of consciousness, what we have here termed the pre-tragic and the tragic. Some people move from level one to level two as a result of lost trust in life, usually occasioned by a personal tragedy. Others move from pre-tragic to tragic because they are witness to the virtually unbearable suffering in the world. The laws and principles they had used to make sense of the world no longer seem sensible. Some individuals, after shifting to tragic consciousness, revert back to pre-tragic. This is either because they find some new, comforting explanation for their suffering (based on a superficial reworking of their old beliefs), or because they simply forget their experience of tragedy and fall back into their prior pre-tragic state.

But there is a third level that is available at the leading edge of consciousness. We call this level "post-tragic." Here, the person or culture is able to once again participate in the elemental joy of living. This happens when the individual (or culture) is able to reconnect to the core Eros and aliveness of reality. In "A Dialogue of Self and Soul," Yeats wrote of this third level, post-tragic consciousness, in the understated but raw Eros of his verse. Here is an example:

When such as I cast out remorse
So great a sweetness flows into the breast
We must laugh and we must sing
We are blest by everything
Everything we look upon is blest.

What causes the emergence of this third level of consciousness is always the deepening into what we might call emotional maturity or wisdom. Part of it may come from depth work that the person has done with his or her own wounds. Another part comes from the maturity of letting go and letting God. Often the source is the evolution of a more poignant and potent worldview. But it always comes from some process of joyful deepening.

These same three levels of consciousness apply to the sexual. There is pre-tragic sexuality, tragic sexuality, and post-tragic sexuality. Pre-tragic sexuality has three major expressions:

The first form of pre-tragic sexuality is purely animal sexuality—a physical, instinctual impulse unburdened by human values or narratives. This is the human attempt to partake in the purely animal mode of sexuality, which we will term "the sex-neutral narrative." It does not work because it is basically regressive. While embracing the animal is essential for our sexuality, it is not enough. Most of us experience the sexual as being more than only physical.

The second form of the pre-tragic sexual is sexuality defined by the laws, strictures, and taboos of religion. Sexuality is pre-tragic in this context because it is clear. Sex in every particular circumstance is either allowed and embraced or forbidden and rejected. Often the religious view is sex negative, but sometimes (for the sake of having children or even companionship), sex is considered positive or even sacred. But it is pre-tragic because it is fully understood. Sex has its place, its boundaries, and its permissions. All is explained. Everything is on firm ground. At this level of sexuality, we deploy law, culture, and taboo to sublimate the sexual and redirect its force to support our committed relationships. We further invest its power as the animating force in our cultural creations. At this level of consciousness, we feel the need to construct vessels of commitment that are sufficient to hold the raw, anarchic power and seductive beauty of the sexual. But this level remains pre-tragic because it is clear to us through laws and customs that are correct and therefore constitute the most right and righteous approach to the sexual.

The third expression of pre-tragic sexuality is sex that occurred in the West during and in the years immediately following the sexual revolution. Most of the old sexual ways were overturned. For most people, sex no longer needed to be tightly linked to marriage to make it proper and good. The contraceptive pill broke the causal link between sex and children. A new world was born. The sexual revolution gave us the sex-positive narrative. But it was pre-tragic because—like the sex-negative narrative—it boasted an uncomplicated clarity about sex. But all was not sweetness and light. The bland, pre-tragic, sex-positive narrative of the sexual revolution could not hold.

from pre-tragic to tragic sex

Many of us today remain largely ensconced in pre-tragic sex. For some of us, that is because we are blithely positive about sex. Our arousal arouses in us virtually no ambivalence or complexity. Others remain pre-tragic because we live firmly within the boundaries of classical religious strictures around sexuality. Even if they are defined largely in their breach, the boundaries are clear. Our actions may be conflicted, but our frameworks remain cogent. We may be both sinners and saints, but we have a clear understanding of what it means to sin and what it means to be saintly.

But for a large swath of people in the Western world, pre-tragic sexuality is over. A second level of consciousness around sex has emerged. We have moved from the pre-tragic sexual to the tragic sexual. The sexual revolution gave way to a world in which sex is no longer innocent. Hidden issues of sexual abuse, sexual violence, and sexual harassment have come to the surface. On the one hand, there is a dramatic evolution of consciousness. A line is drawn in the culture that says, "No more harassment and no more violence." Indeed, before the mid-1970s, even the words "sexual harassment" were not part of our lexicon and certainly not part of our laws. In the West the ascendancy of the feminine in education and in the workforce brought in its wake a vital new vigilance that says no to any form of sexual boundary-crossing that is not welcomed by both parties. This is an important step in healing the deep violation of the feminine that has characterized much of Western history.

And yet there is a loss of clarity around sexuality. With the loss of clarity comes a loss of innocence coupled with a new form of free-floating anxiety and even fear surrounding sex. We might even venture to say that there is a new puritanism in relationship to the sexual. The old sex-negative positions of religion seem to have covertly resurfaced in the campaigns against sexual harassment.

Now to be clear, we all agree that numerous forms of harassment and sexual violence were rampant in the pre-tragic sexual world. Even in the world of sexual revolution, sexual harassment remained a given. Black Power leader

Stokely Carmichael famously remarked that the "right position for women in the Black Panthers is prone." Marital rape was legal virtually everywhere. Rape in war was regarded as the spoils of the victors. Sexual enslavement of women of "inferior" culture or religion was common throughout the world. What we would today call sexual harassment or abuse was considered to be relatively normal.

Nonetheless, most men did not harass, were not sexually violent, did not rape, and did not abuse women. The horrific lack of legal strictures allowed the actions of a small minority of men to inflict great pain and to poison the sexual culture of the world. The evolution of love that raised consciousness and made all these forms of sexual violation unacceptable, both legally and socially, is a desperately necessary and long-overdue advance. But a strong fragrance of the old anti-sexual puritanism seems to have crept its way into today's sexual discourse. Legal scholars and social critics alike have pointed out that in the early days of the war on sexual harassment, the core issue was harassment. As years went by, how- ever, the emphasis shifted to the sexual. Major cases of significant harassment with no sexual component were let off the hook, while any case that had even a whiff of the sexual was treated with full severity. Sex, once again, was bad.

The anti-sexual theme is covert, sensed but not articulated in the public mind. This is where the move from pre-tragic to tragic begins to emerge. We no longer have a clear sexual narrative. We are confused by sexuality. We are not sure whether we are living in the golden age of sex or in a rape culture. Rape on campus, date rape, and confusion about what constitutes consent—when does yes mean yes and when does no mean no - abound. Regret is not rape, and arousal is not consent, yet all too often they are confused. The hook-up culture of emotionally unattached sex dominates the campus mythos, yet very few college students say they feel sexually fulfilled or liberated. Women feel prude-shamed for not being willing to hook up and then slut-shamed for hooking up.

The anti-sexual attitude is covert. In so many dimensions of our culture, puritanism lives side by side with promiscuity. How else might we explain the national obsession with sexual scandal, such as the affair between Bill Clinton and Monica Lewinsky? The insatiable appetite of Americans for sexual titillation, combined with the fascination with public degradation and shaming around sex, virtually demanded that newspapers—driven by the race for advertising dollars—cover the details of the scandal more than any other event in the world for a period of nearly two years.

Today there are no clear guidelines and even fewer clear values regarding sex. It is true that we're seeing a long-overdue and welcome increase in sexual ethics. We have significantly less tolerance for all varieties of sexual harassment and violence. Yet the new sexual ethics are not rooted in a new sexual ethos. There is no sexual narrative that both dignifies and eroticizes our lives.

Hardly anyone is really happy with sex. If they are, it's only in the first wave of the sexual encounter when the passion is high and the egos are low. After that, most everyone feels like they are not quite getting enough, getting it right, or getting to move on when they are ready. And if they are getting some, they suspect it should be better than it is. Most everyone is quietly convinced that it is so much better for everybody else. Everyone is obsessed with that mythical couple, living somewhere in New Jersey, who are madly in love and having great sex after two decades of marriage. No one, of course, has ever met them, but reported sightings regularly crop up in magazines, talk shows, and self-help books. We live with the rampant dissatisfaction produced by the great tease of sexual satisfaction, which for the first time in history seems to be democratized. Everyone feels entitled, but virtually no one feels fulfilled.

shadow dance

sexual shadows

But if all that were not enough, sex is also a big-time killer. Men are raping men and killing men over sex. Men are killing women in domestic violence scenes. In the world arena, men still use sex in war to break down the social order and humiliate their enemies. While the term "rape culture" has been powerfully critiqued, more than a million rapes occur every year, leaving irrevocable damage on the lives of women and men. There is a powerful and important literature that suffuses culture which calls men out on this particular form of masculine shadow.

But don't think that women are off the hook. The feminine shadow has women killing men over sex. According to extensive rigorous data, gathered by leading cultural critics Cathy Young and Warren Farrell, the level of domestic violence inflicted by women on men is equal to that inflicted by men on women. The literature of abuse reminds us that women are also killing men in domestic violence scenes. At its heart, virtually all domestic violence is connected to wounds around sexuality. Women also engage in what has been described alternatively as social murder or name rape. The early feminists were right when they said that the rape of a name is also rape. For example, to be falsely accused of rape or sexual assault, and to have those kinds of accusations disseminated over the internet, where lies live forever, is a devastating experience. In this tragic scenario, name rape is reenacted every day online. We interviewed women who had been raped and also had brothers, sons, or partners who were subject to this kind of severe name rape. According to these women—all with powerful feminist sensibilities—both are equally egregious.

Often false sexual complaints cluster together when a group of women (or men in the more classical lynch mob) bypass structures of investigation and justice in order to socially murder someone. For example, groups of women who feel rejected and hurt—finding out, as feminist writer Jessica Roemischer writes, "that they are not the only one"—may get together and use false or distorted accusations of sexual misconduct to socially kill a man.

In the internet age, disaffected people find each other more easily. Sometimes that is constructive and positive, specifically when the disaffected have been genuinely victimized. At other times, however, people who gather together via the internet and other social structures manifest more of a moblike energy or group-think mentality. They incite each other's anger. Facts and ulterior motives are never checked or cross-checked and social lynching takes place on the web.

Malice is not limited to males. There is masculine shadow and feminine shadow. Feminist writer Hanna Rosin devotes a chilling chapter in her book The End of Men to feminine violence. Feminist writers like Daphne Patai, Katie Roiphe, Laura Kipnis, and Christina Hoff Sommers have long warned of the growing phenomenon of false sexual complaints by women. Of course the sexual shadows at play which generate malice are often hidden. As Milan Kundera reminded us, "malice can never admit to itself so it must plead other motives." As Patai and other writers point out, name rape hides its true intention under the veneer of victim advocacy. The perpetrator is usually disguised either as a victim or as a rescuer who is "protecting other women." There is always some politically correct formula used to cover up wounded ego and genuine hurt, which get lethally mixed with the often strange bedfellows of malice, envy, self-interest, and self-protection. The fig leaf of relatively minor sexual hurt in the normal arc of human relationships often masks the infliction of lethal hurt that is exponentially more destructive by many orders. All of this is part of the confusion of sexuality's tragic phase.

The confusion itself is the source of much of our devastation. It is the loss of clarity that moves us from pre-tragic to tragic sex. The tragic sexual leaves so many mortally wounded in its wake. There is so much pain from something that should be the source of so much pleasure.

All of these phenomena that are rampant in our culture are expressions of the tragic sexual. But that is just the tip of the iceberg. We have not even begun to explore the super complex territory of monogamy, the myth of the white picket fence, polyamory, open marriage, betrayal in its many forms, the great controversy surrounding "recovered" memories, post-facto reinterpretations of old sexual experience, the claims of rape culture, and the list goes on and on. And anyone who, God forbid, does not want the same kind of sex that the majority approves of is in big trouble. Same-sex couples struggle, transgendered couples struggle, and anyone with any kind of alternative sexual drive has a rough start even before the pleasure actually begins and ends. The confusion around all of these issues is simply an expression of level-two tragic sexuality.

There is more than a little that is tragic in the contemporary sexual landscape. We are not sure about anything. Either God is more than slightly sadistic with a significant interest in teasing and even torturing us through the ordeal of sex or in some mysterious way it is the essential key to this whole life journey. We are not sure. Our lack of clarity drains our energy, robs us of passion, saps our vitality, and de-eroticizes our lives.

Given all of the above, along with the fact that our yearning for great sex is such a desperate and central issue in our lives, it stands to reason that the divine designer who set up this ultimate tease must be a flaming asshole. Or worse still, there is no designer, all is random and chance, and there is no "true north" or meaning in our sexuality. It will always be this hopelessly confused. That is the tragic view.

Or, possibility two: the inherent intelligence of the self-organizing universe totally and absolutely rocks. The love intelligence of the cosmos so desires our good that she wanted to place the deepest wisdom necessary to navigate our lives with power and passion right in the center of our experience—in the heart of our sexuality—just to make sure we did not miss it. That's why all wisdom about life was encoded in the sexual. That realization moves us toward the post-tragic view of sexuality.

from the tragic to post-tragic sexual

We are lost in the tragic sexual, searching for a new narrative. We long for a return to sexual innocence. Not a pre-tragic innocence but a post-tragic innocence. We yearn to re-virginate. We are not seeking sexual license as much as we desperately yearn for a return to Eros. We yearn to live the erotic life. We want to live in an erotic society. To return to Eros, we need a new sexual narrative. Core to this new narrative must be a precise and potent understanding of the relationship between the sexual and the erotic. Are they the same or are they different? If they are different, how do they interact with one another? Could it be that our sexuality is collapsing because we have lost contact with Eros? Could it be that when we look to sex to fulfill all of our erotic needs, sex collapses under the weight of a burden that it cannot possibly bear? Is our confused pathos around the sexual actually rooted in the urgent need for a new sexual narrative that clarifies the shocking relationship among the erotic, the sexual, and the sacred?

Until such a narrative emerges, we will weirdly vacillate between being puritans and libertines on alternative days or even during different hours of the same day. We are politically correct during the day while yearning to be sexually incorrect at night. Sexual anthropologist Esther Perel reminds us, somewhat sardonically, that we often demonstrate in daytime against the kinds of sexuality that we yearn for at night. We need a new post-tragic story of sex and Eros.

beyond Marcuse and Brown : a return to eros

Herbert Marcuse and Norman O. Brown are the two great social philosophers who, in the latter half of the twentieth century, sought to reclaim a vision of Eros that might form the basis of a new human and a new society. But both of them lacked a sufficiently potent worldview from which that new vision of Eros could emerge. Marcuse was lost in the neo-Marxist restructuring of society, which failed to honor the potential, creative Eros of free markets and an emergent conscious capitalism. Brown sought to reclaim a regressive Dionysian innocence by recovering key stands in Freud's more mythical thinking, while recasting and rejecting still other dimensions of Freud.

Today it is clear that whatever their crucial contributions, neither neo-Marxism nor psychoanalysis is the fertile ground from which a new erotic worldview will arise.

In this work it has been our tender and audacious intention to articulate just such a new erotic worldview. We tried to tell a new story about sex whose subplot is the powerful relationship among the sexual, the erotic, and the sacred. We retold the story of love, distinguishing between outrageous and ordinary love. We articulated a new meta meme: The Universe is a Love Story. We are convinced that this worldview is a sufficient basis to catalyze a return to Eros and a sexual narrative that is an affront to shame. Our vision of Eros is rooted in a spiritual, mystical, scientific, evolutionary worldview, which understands that all of reality is allurement, and which experiences the sexual as an expression of the erotic evolutionary impulse that moves all of reality. In this worldview, rooted in the best science and spirituality available on the planet at this moment in time, the sexual is the seat of all wisdom.

In this new narrative, Eros is not merely ordinary love, which human egos deploy as a strategy to achieve security and status. Rather, Eros is the outrageous love, which moves the sun and the stars, which is the very heart of existence itself. When we awaken to the Eros of evolution alive within us, we awaken as outrageous lovers. Our model for outrageous love is none other than the sexual itself. The sexual models the erotic ; it does not exhaust the erotic. The erotic and the holy are one. This is the core of the post-tragic narrative of sexuality that will allow us to move beyond the pervasive sexual shame that covertly suffuses our culture and is the root of so much suffering and pain. This new sexual narrative is the necessary basis of a new sexual politics of Eros that has the potency and power to take us all home.

sources for the new narrative

We draw the new narrative from several sources. Systems theory, evolutionary theory, and science are crucial sources. Various schools of psychology, integral theory, attachment theory, and the social sciences all contribute significantly. But the core wellspring from which we drink is a great Hebrew mystery tradition. Mysteries are meant to remain esoteric, secret. Therefore, allow us to share with you why in our generation it is both permitted and even a sacred obligation to share these mysteries.

We live in an age when ancient wisdoms, long relegated to the basements of the spirit, are being reclaimed. The Zohar, the magnum opus of Hebrew mysticism, teaches that our era is the one in which the "gates of wisdom will be opened." For the first time, after several eons of intense spiritual evolution, we have the vessels to hold the light of the ancient secrets. The mystics suggest that we may well be able to hold the light more deeply today than even the ancients for whom the wisdom was initially intended. It is only now, after the vessels of law, science, and ethics have been integrated into our psyches, that we can go back and fully reclaim Eros and enchantment. It is in the service of the great Hebrew Goddess of Eros (Shechinah) that we enter the mysteries.

We, the co-authors of Return to Eros, are—or at least aspire to be—erotic mystics. We study, teach, and try to live the sacred erotic texts in our lives. The think tank of which we, Marc and Kristina, are, respectively, president and board director, is committed to envisioning and evolving the future of Eros in every field of human endeavor. The Outrageous Love Project (www.OutrageousLove.com) and the Integral Evolutionary Tantra School (www.IntegralEvolutionaryTantra.com) are two projects that emerged from the Center, which we were delighted to cofound. Both projects are committed to articulating a next-stage vision of Eros and ethics, which humbly and audaciously evolve the source code of culture and consciousness.

The mystery texts of the ancient Solomon lineage Eros, as well as those of other spiritually incorrect traditions, have been our guides and friends for many years. Of course, like all mystics who engage sacred wisdom, we hear the text in accord with the inner melody of our souls. We now share this song with you in the form of this book. You are invited to find the place in your soul where you can receive and integrate this ancient wisdom into your own song.

Dr. Marc Gafni and Dr. Kristina Kincaid
Northeast Kingdom, Vermont

The Cosmo-Erotic Universe

a new sexual narrative

If you stop to think even for a short moment, you realize that sex really is the great mystery of our lives. This is truer today than it was in any previous generation. For we have lost the story line of meaning around our sexuality. There are four basic stories about sex that we have inherited in our culture, and none of them addresses our sexual experience. These hand-me-down narratives can loosely be labeled as sex negative, sex positive, sex neutral, and sex sacred.

sex negative

The sex-negative narrative is articulated in our culture to prevent us from having sex. They tell us, of course, that it is for our own protection. According to this narrative, sex is somehow wrong, immoral, or sinful. The spokespeople for sex negative are quite potent. Even when we think we have gotten free of them, they pop up again inside our hearts or heads, wagging their fingers disapprovingly. Even if we have successfully removed them from our minds and psyches, they still show up in the way our bodies respond and behave. And, of course, they remind us constantly of all the trouble sex has gotten the world into—from the Trojan War to the Clinton/Lewinsky drama. Not to mention the trouble it has gotten us into—emotionally, psychologically, personally, professionally, and physically. It's all the fault of sex.

You have to admit that the sexual renunciates and conservatives have a point. If you want to keep life simple, clean, and orderly, foregoing or limiting the sexual experience might be an excellent decision. If you like spiritual

eros

exercises—and you are up for it—take a few minutes and write down all the times sex got you into trouble in any or all of the above areas. We predict you will probably generate quite a list.

Lots of religious and conventional moralists fall into the sex-negative category. Religion typically affirms love and passion as virtues but divorces them entirely from sex. Moralist religion works hard to erect boundaries that will protect us from the pitfalls of our sexuality.

But the sex-negative narrative, while it certainly has a point, clearly does not fully capture our experience of the sexual. While we all know that sex requires a dimension of discipline—context and commitment matter for sure—most of us know in our hearts that the moralists are wrong and that sex is ultimately, and overwhelmingly, good. And it's not merely a side benefit of (or a tool for achieving) a loving relationship. As the fourteenth-century Zen master Ikkyu observed:

> *With a young beauty, sporting in deep love play;*
> *We sit in the pavilion, a pleasure girl and this Zen*
> *monk. Enraptured by hugs and kisses,*
> *I certainly don't feel as if I am burning in hell.*

sex positive

This brings us to the second story about sex that we hear in our culture: the sex-positive narrative. This story is told by a powerful coalition of forces talking about sex. This group tells us, "Sex is wonderful. If liberated, it's the panacea for all ills; if repressed, it's the source of all dysfunction." Sexual revolutionaries, Freudians in disguise, along with many other intelligent folk and proponents of schools of modern psychology, work hard to strip sex of anything remotely spiritual or even emotional. They want to liberate sex from love, from Eros, and from the myriad existential and emotional complexities. To these individuals, sex is simply positive.

Truth be told, Freud himself was the most influential modern cheerleader at this party. Rooted in a hydraulic model of the psyche, which slightly confuses human beings and steam engines, he taught us that if we could just find a way to release sexual tension in a balanced way, we would be healthy and happy. The problem with this narrative is that, though we may be having much more sex, we are not feeling much more positive.

In fact, after engaging in all of the sex that so many generations thought would signal heaven on earth, we are shocked to find that the same feelings of alienation, depression, and emptiness still plague us. Okay—hydraulic equilibrium achieved—what are we supposed to feel when the sexual revolution failed to bring us any closer to liberation? We remain mired in suffering, just as before.

sex neutral

This brings us to the third sexual narrative: sex is neither positive nor negative. The third sexual story is the sex-neutral narrative. This story was articulated by a host of sex researchers, perhaps most prominent the highly controversial, but highly impactful, Alfred Kinsey. Kinsey's father was a fundamentalist Christian who raised his son squarely in the sex-negative camp. Kinsey rebelled, however. Receiving his PhD in biology from Harvard, he argued that sex is simply a neutral biological mechanism. He sought, in both his personal and professional life, to completely disinhibit sex from any sense of being either negative or positive. For Kinsey and the sexual story he put into our culture, sex—all forms of it without exception—is simply biology. "So let's get over all of these inhibitions. Why all the fuss about it anyway?"

The problem with this third narrative is that, like the sex-negative philosophy, it does not fully capture our sexual experience. Sex just does not feel neutral to us. Having sex and having dinner just are not the same. But that's not all. The more neutral we make sex, and the more we make it available, like food, the less satisfied we are. Uninhibited sex is available in infinite variety in almost every imaginable social or commercial context, and yet we do not seem any the better for it. So much sex and so little pleasure. So many orgasms and so little fulfillment.

A few decades ago, a sociologist named David Riesman called sex "the last frontier." If this is true, then we have crossed it and found it wanting. Psychologists report that patients rarely complain about sexual dysfunction or repression anymore (what seemed to be the most common complaint in the days of Freud). Rather, the malaise of our time is the lack of feeling or passion and a disconnect between sex and spirit. Sex is all around, and yet it is hard to tell whether anyone is truly enhanced by it. Indeed, no one even seems to be really enjoying themselves—at least not in any sort of sustained manner.

T. S. Eliot describes this state of affairs in his epic poem "The Waste Land":

She turns and looks a moment in the glass,
Hardly aware of her departed lover;

Eliot speaks of the hidden alienation from the sexual even after the Church's sexual mores have been overturned.

Her brain allows one half-formed thought to pass;
"Well, now that's done: and I'm glad it's over."

The alienation sets in the moment it's over, surfacing our discomfort with our own sexing.

When lovely woman stoops to folly and
Paces about her room again, alone,

We pace—unable to rest in what should be the aftertaste—our confusion around sex darkening what should have been the afterglow.

She smoothes her hair with automatic hand,
And puts a record on the gramophone.

sex sacred

The fourth sexual story, often deployed as a counter to the sex-neutral narrative, is sex sacred. Rooted in certain strains of the great religions, this narrative claims that sex is not negative, neutral, or even positive. Rather, it is holy. The evidence of sex's holiness, the sex-sacred story, is taken to be self-evident. Sex creates life, life is holy, therefore sex is holy.

That is a pretty good argument as far as it goes. But again, it does not address our full experience of sexuality. Just ask yourself: is most of the sex that you have for the sake of procreation? For most people, most of the time, most of their sex has nothing to do with making babies. So to root the sex-sacred narrative in sex for babies just does not speak to the truth of our full sexual lives. Besides all of that, are we really sure what we mean when we talk about sex or anything else as sacred or holy? We know it means that sex is not just neutral or even merely positive. But what does "sacred" really mean, anyway?

a new sexual narrative: sex erotic

So although all four of the sexual narratives contain some elemental validity, they are, at best, true but incomplete. They each may be spiritually and politically correct in their respective cultural space, but they do not address our deepest knowing and yearnings about sex.

We need a new sexual narrative. We need a new story. Enter the philosophy of sex erotic. This fifth sexual story, the one that addresses most fully our sexual experience, is that sex is indeed sacred but not only when it creates children. Sex is not sacred only because it creates life. Sex is sacred because it is life. Sex is the very pulse of life itself. Sex is the fundamental nature of all existence. Therefore, sex is the ultimate guide to living in alignment with all of reality. Let us call this new sexual narrative "sex erotic."

If sex is life, then naturally sex is the seat of all wisdom about life. Sex is not only our great delight and pleasure—sex is our ultimate teacher about living. For life itself is, at its core, Eros.

sex models eros

The paradox of this book is that it is all about sex and not about sex at all. Sex is life. But if we are only alive in our sex, then we are already dead. By contrast, being fully alive in the sexual models for us what it means to be radically alive in every facet of life. The experience of being radically alive is called Eros. To be fully alive in every dimension of your life is what it means to live an erotic life.

That is why we have termed the new sexual narrative "sex erotic." Sex erotic suggests that sex and Eros are not to be collapsed synonyms. Sex and Eros are different but closely related terms. Sex is sex. Eros is the radical aliveness that animates and drives all of reality. The new sexual narrative of sex erotic informs us of two great truths. First, that sex is the expression of the evolutionary Eros that animates and drives all of reality, awake and alive in us. Second, that sex models for us what it means to live in Eros in every facet of our existence.

The purpose of this book is to articulate the new sexual narrative. Sex is neither negative nor neutral nor merely positive. Sex is not even just sacred because it creates life. The new narrative is that sex is life. That's why our aliveness is most directly accessed through sex. To be sexual is to be alive, and to be alive is to be sexual, but our basic yearning is not just to be fully alive during sex but also to be radically alive in all parts of our life. It is this voice of authentic yearning that is our most reliable spiritual guide. To be radically alive in every part of our life is what it means to live in Eros.

What, then, is the relationship of sex to Eros? The answer is as profound as it is simple: sex models Eros. But sex does not exhaust Eros. Sex models what it means to live an erotic life in every arena of your engagement. To be radically alive means much more than simply being sexual. To be erotic only in sex is to live a deadened life of quiet desperation. Sex erotic implies that sex—when it is lived in its fullest form—incarnates Eros even as it models Eros. Sex erotic teaches us how to live in Eros, not only in sex but also in all the nonsexual dimensions of our lives. That is what it means to live an erotic life.

Eros is aliveness. Aliveness occurs as you, when the energy of reality awakens in you and through you. Eros is the vitality that pulses through our atomic structure, making our protons and electrons dance in perpetual ecstasy. Eros is the passion that makes our cells and atoms yearn for each other, always allured and constantly sexing. Eros is what makes us want to dance. Eros is—very literally—what transforms a relationship from a strategy for security to an event of cosmic significance. You can be sexually active and in relationship and remain profoundly lonely. It is only when you realize that your own attractions and allurements participate in the attraction and allurement that is the very structure of the cosmos that you begin to live an erotic life.

In the lived sensuality of an erotic life, loneliness makes no sense. Loneliness is the opposite of Eros and aliveness. Eros is wholeness and interconnectivity. It is the essential nature of a cosmos whose core truth might well be: reality is relationship. It is only when you realize that reality is relationship and that your relationship is part of the grand cacophony of relationship at every level of the cosmos that you truly transcend loneliness.

When you really get the scientific truth that your erotic autobiography is an intended outcome of the love intelligence of reality, then you begin to be at home in your life. The scientific reality of your radical uniqueness is shocking when you really get it. You have an irreducibly unique atomic and cellular signature. The extent and precision of your intricate uniqueness is made clearer every day with new studies and evidence. Your level of dazzling uniqueness intuitively implies intention. When you know that you are personally addressed and intended, you fall in love with your life. Your heart beats faster, and your eyes open wider. You realize that the ache of your wetness or the throbbing of your fullness is reality awake as you. The truly alive person does

cello

not know the ennui of boredom. Everything is fascinating to the person who is truly alive. It matters not whether it's a piercing pain, a moment of pleasure, a bucket of grief, or a glimpse of beauty.

the meaning of eros

Eros is the principle of aliveness and magic inherent in all of reality. Something infinitely real animates everything. Reality is realness, which is another way of saying Eros or aliveness. Everything radiates an intense aliveness. The intensification of aliveness is the natural result of living an erotic life. Most people have had the experience of visiting a place and finding it vibrating with aliveness, color, and immediacy. Some years later they may visit the same place again and find it drab and dreary. Most likely it is not the place that has changed, but the person. Beauty is always in the eye of the beholder. When your eyes are alive, then the hills are alive. When your eyes are asleep, then even the most beautiful vista is deadened.

Our lives are a search for passionate aliveness. Our lives are a search for Eros. We remember well Eros lost. Until we are able to recover Eros, we are filled with an inconsolable longing that can be healed by no external balm.

We hunger for the depths of aliveness, for it is only from those depths that we are capable of love. It is only in the quivering of aliveness that we are capable of being all we can be. That is what it means to be holy. The opposite of holy is not unholy. The opposite of holy is superficial. The holy is the real. We long for what is real. That is why we yearn with all of our being to return to Eros.

not synonymous

When we talk about Eros or the erotic, we suffer from any number of confusions. There's an important relationship between the erotic and the sexual, but as we said above, they're not the same thing. Eros is the essential aliveness of reality—it's the experience of being on the inside, like when you're running and at some point you break through and you're in the zone or the inside of experience.

There is a fullness of presence in Eros and a feeling that your yearning participates in the evolutionary yearning of being. In Eros you have a felt experience that you are not separate; you experience your own interconnectivity with the larger context, with the wholeness of it all. All blessings flow from Eros. The goodness of life, the color in a black-and-white world, and all ethics flow through the channels of Eros. The loss of Eros is the failure of ethics. Creativity, intimacy and relationship, politics, economics—nothing moves without the erotic. When there's a disconnect from Eros, systems begin to break down both in the world of the personal and in the world of the collective.

When you feel fully alive, when you are in Eros, there is no question about the meaning of life. When you are in Eros, there is no question about the essential goodness of life. When you live in Eros, life is self-evidently meaningful and obviously good. Here is an example of how sex models Eros: when you are on the edge of orgasm, you are on the inside of life—yearning, totally present, ultimately connected, lost in the experience, and yet most radically your Unique Self. When you are in Eros, you have no questions about the meaning of life. You are life.

At the edge of sexual explosion, you do not stop in the middle to contemplate philosophical issues or life's meaning, nor do you question the natural goodness of life. You are fully alive and fully in it. In fact, those five qualities—living on the inside, fullness of presence, yearning, wholeness and interconnectivity, and the experience of your unique identity—are the first five of the twelve faces of Eros that we will be exploring in this book. "Sex models Eros" means that sex models the experience of being on the inside, fully present and connected, deeply yearning, and ultimately yourself, in every facet of your life.

ancient articulations

For ancient articulations of this new sexual narrative, we turn to the hidden wisdom of the spiritually incorrect masters. These masters taught the esoteric traditions of all the great systems of spirit. They are the erotic mystics. The esoteric name for this tradition in the earlier sources is "the Secret of the Cherubs." We will meet the cherubs formally in chapter three. For now, a brief introduction will suffice.

The cherubs are two figures that live atop the Ark of the Covenant in Solomon's temple in Jerusalem. According to the sacred text, the voice of God "speaks from between the two cherubs." What is not known other than to initiates in the esoteric tradition is that these two cherubs are locked in ecstatic sexual embrace. The voice of God speaks from between the sexually entwined cherubs.

The spiritually incorrect Tantric masters were not limited to the Erotic mystics of the Solomon lineage. They appeared in different guises in all the great traditions. Their true teachings were always esoteric, hidden from public access. Only the initiates truly understood their radical intention. These masters are called the Kabbalists in Judaism, and the Tantric masters in Hinduism and Buddhism. Rumi and Hafiz in Sufism were initiates, as were the Cathars in mystical Christianity. One master of the Zen tradition was named Ikkyu. Mary Magdalene was a master in the hidden Christian tradition. We add to these ancient traditions a vital modern wisdom tradition that we will refer to as Evolutionary Spirituality. This contemporary wisdom lineage is rooted in evolutionary science, systems science, modern physics, biology, chaos theory, and complexity theory.

Veiled in all of these great traditions is a hidden, subversive, mystical teaching. It is either ignored or reinterpreted to avoid its full implications. The great teachers were literally killed, socially murdered, or otherwise sidelined from positions of influence. They were destroyed because the fear of Eros overwhelmed both the goodness of Eros and the wisdom of Eros.

The ancient religions, in their public teachings, sought to impose a measure of order and stability on the ignorant masses. To do so, sex had to be controlled before anything else. This is the legitimate reason for the sex-negative teaching of the great religions. Today, what we need most desperately, however, is not to control sex. Rather, we need to reinvest our sex with a meaning and purpose that is equal to the central role that sex plays in our lives. We have killed all the gods except for Aphrodite, the goddess of sex. It is in the sexual that we still hear the murmuring of the sacred. But we cannot quite make out the words. We need to articulate a new sexual story. We need a story that invests not only our sex but all of our life with fresh aliveness and a new plot line of meaning.

The source of this narrative is in the spiritually incorrect teachings, which understood implicitly that embedded in the sexual, in the full panoply of its gorgeous and graphic detail, is all that is holy, all that is wise, and all that is good. The masters of spiritually incorrect Tantra viewed the sexual act itself as the great wisdom mystery reflecting all the deepest truths of the spirit. In a world torn apart by fanatic fundamentalisms and insipid liberalisms, we need a new teaching that all of us can recognize and take home.

Contrary to conventional religion and much of psychology, the post-conventional, spiritually incorrect Tantric masters insisted that sex is integrally related to love and Eros. There is no disconnect. And not because it is nice, secure, and comfortable if you are able to love the person you are sleeping with. But far more powerfully—and this is the heart of the secret—because the sexual is the ultimate model for Eros and love. The erotic and the holy are one. In every ethical sexual encounter, one can create an energetic container for the sacred, for opening up fully and absolutely into the radical aliveness and love that are already there. The sexual in all of her intricate detail is a most potent teacher, ripping us open, if we will but let her, to the radical fullness of spirit that seeks our pleasure and goodness.

One thirteenth-century Kabbalist put it this way: "Whoever has not desired a woman is like an ass and even less than an ass, for it is from the sexual one understands divine service."

Or in the language of Zen master Ikkyu:

Rinzai's disciples never got the Zen message,
But I, the Blind Donkey, know the truth:
Love play can make you immortal.
The autumn breeze of a single night of love is better than a hundred thousand years of sterile sitting meditation...

And just in case he was being too subtle, and to avoid being piously misinterpreted, Ikkyu continues:

Stilted koans and convoluted answers are all monks have, Pandering endlessly to officials and rich patrons.
Good friends of the Dharma, so proud, let me tell you,
A brothel girl in gold brocade is worth more than any of you,
Emerging from the world's grime,
a puritan saint is still nowhere near a Buddha.
Enter a brothel and Great Wisdom will explode upon you.
Manjushri should have let Ananda enjoy himself in the whorehouse –
Now he will never know the joys of elegant love play.

Sex stands as the ultimate symbol, both signifying and actually modeling the sacred wisdom, which needs to animate and guide all areas of life. The goal of life is to live erotically in all facets of being, and sex is the model par excellence for sacred erotic living in all of the nonsexual arenas that make up most of our lives. The sexual is in the hidden teaching of the spiritually incorrect Tantric masters. It is the ultimate spiritual master. Thus, deep understanding of the sexual is the ultimate guide to accessing the spirit in every dimension of our reality.

We are not talking about sexual technique. Even when important, sexual technique is technical at best. Sexual technique can never make you a great lover. You can only be a great lover if you are fully alive. To be a great lover in all facets of your being, you must listen deeply to the simple yet elegant spirit whisperings of the sexual. Nietzsche, the great German philosopher, got something right when he said, "The degree and kind of man's sexuality reaches up into the topmost summit of his spirit."

sex is the answer

Is there anything except sex that so grabs our rapt attention; incessantly pursues us; and occupies our daydreams, fantasies, and yearnings? The mystics are just stating the obvious when they say that, with sex, God is trying to GET OUR ATTENTION. "Hello... over here! Pay attention!" Now we are not talking about the God who sends good people to burn in hell because they slipped up on one of his impossible demands. Nor even the Grandfather in heaven who hands out chocolate to do-gooders. Forget that God. The God you don't believe in doesn't exist. Rather, the God that exists for us is the personal, erotic life force that courses through reality and knows our name. The God we believe in is the vitality of an intelligent Eros that initiates, animates, and drives all of reality and addresses us personally. The God we believe in is the force for healing and transformation in the world. The God who knows our name is the God who so clearly calls out to us that sex is the answer.

When religion splits us off from our sexuality, we correctly intuit that something is deeply askew. But sex is not a panacea. Sex is not a drug that will soothe away the lurking feeling of ennui and that this cannot be all there is. Good orgasms will not a good life make. Sex is also not merely neutral or simply sacred because it is the method of procreation. Rather, sex is the answer as a model and not as the sum total of all Eros, holiness, and wisdom. Sex, if we will but listen, is a great master of the spirit—better than any guru, psychologist, rabbi, or priest. Sex can teach us how to reclaim the erotic in every nonsexual aspect and element of our lives. For Eros is not sex. The sexual models the erotic; it does not exhaust the erotic.

erotic and nonerotic sex

When we say that sex models Eros, we are not talking about the merely sexual. We are talking about erotic sex. The merely sexual involves a few pathetic grunts, maybe an occasional kiss and nice word, the titillation of the narrow section of the genitals for a few minutes at the most, and a brief fleeting pleasure at climax. If you are lost in mere sex, then you will never penetrate and never be penetrated.

We all know that titillation of the sexual instruments feels good. That is not, however, the sum total of Eros. Superficial feeling good is for people who are afraid of the full divine power of the erotic sexual. When the sexual awakens as the erotic sexual, it takes on an entirely different quality of power, potency, and pleasure. Sex is not a path unless it cracks you open to the divine.

People cling to the outside of the sexual, to breasts and pallid orgasms, because they are afraid to open up to the full power of Eros. It is the fear of Eros that keeps most people fixated on pathetic titillation. Sex invites us to be open as love. Not as ordinary love but as outrageous love. Outrageous love is Eros. The Erotic mystics of the Solomon lineage teach together with Ikkyu that the universe in every second is always making love. The Kabbalists call it ***zivug***. In this world, the incarnation of that divine movement, the perpetual divine lovemaking, is not ordinary sex but erotic sex. Enter into the inside of sex, and you will find God, the sacred lover and gorgeous, divine paramour of the cosmos. The inside of sex is outrageous love. The inside of sex is Eros.

ordinary love and outrageous love

Understanding the distinction between ordinary and outrageous love is the doorway to all that is magical and mysterious both in the cosmos and in life. We need to realize that Sex with a capital S is a love story. Not an ordinary love story, but an outrageous love story, an erotic love story. Because outrageous love is Eros. It is the radical aliveness and purpose that animates and drives all reality on every level of creation, all the way up and all the way down. Ordinary love is an experience of the human personality, which feels separate from all that is, grasping for some measure of security and comfort. Ordinary love is a strategy of the ego desperately fleeing the feeling of lonely desperation.

The Bengali mystic Tagore alluded to the distinction between ordinary and outrageous love when he said, "Love is not mere human sentiment but the heart of existence itself." The love that he called "mere human sentiment" is what we are referring to as ordinary love. The love that he calls "the heart of existence" is what we are calling outrageous love, or Eros. The mystics of the Kabbalah called ordinary love "the love after creation." They called outrageous love "the love before creation." Love after creation is in reaction. It is all too often culturally conditioned and imposed. Love before creation is what the great writer Dante called l'amor che move il sole e l'altre stele, "the love that moves the sun and the other stars." It is the love that moved the Infinite to manifest reality in the explosion of the big bang. It is the love that is the evolutionary impulse driving all reality to higher and higher levels of consciousness and love.

Ordinary love is valid and good, but it is a strategy of the ego. It is a legitimate and even necessary human experience. It may win you comfort and some measure of illusory security, but ordinary love cannot take you home. Home is the experience that there is no place to go because you have already arrived. Home is when you stop seeking the meaning of life because it becomes outrageously self-evident. Home is when you fall in love with your life anew every day. Home is the knowing that every place you go you are being carried. Only outrageous love takes you home. Outrageous love is the dance of allurement and attraction at the very sub-atomic level of existence. Outrageous love is the ceaseless, ecstatic, creative pulsation that drives the entire process of emergence. Outrageous love is the field of allurement, at every level of reality—from atom, to plant, to animal, to human—that holds all creation together.

But outrageous love can become part of your human experience. Living becomes extraordinary when we access outrageous love in the course of what we like to call ordinary life. When you love your beloved not merely as an unconscious strategy of ego but as an expression of the Eros of existence, outrageous love is awakened in you, and your entire experience of life changes. When you hold your beloved's hand with ordinary love, your hand gets clammy rather quickly. You can't quite find the right position, and soon you want to unclasp. When you hold your beloved's hand with outrageous love, you feel like all is perfect and you want the moment to last forever.

Another scenario. Your baby is crying. Pick up the baby with the hands of ordinary love, and the baby continues to cry and fidget, often more intensely than before. But pick up the baby with outrageous love, and the baby literally melts into you. The crying naturally recedes, and the baby falls into a profound and deep state of rest. The infant has been lifted up into the lap of Eros, and she knows it. You feel the bliss of her resting in the depth of your being, which is the Eros of existence—outrageous love itself. This shift inside you, from emptiness to Eros, from ordinary love to outrageous love, is the change that changes everything.

When the very Eros of existence is awakened in you, you are awakening as outrageous love. You become an outrageous lover. You begin to live an erotic life. Sex transforms from the pitiful grasping for fleeting fulfillment that is not working for virtually anyone, to something else entirely. Sex is revealed as the potent prose and poetry of reality itself, incarnate as your body and your desire. Sex is revealed as the love story of all of reality, happening in and as you. Sex is revealed as the source of all wisdom, pointing us toward the erotic and the holy in every dimension of life. It is a virtuous circle. Sex models Eros. You begin to live the erotic life in every dimension of your nonsexual life. As you re-eroticize your life, you are personally transformed. At the same time, regular sex transforms into erotic sex. Ordinary sex becomes outrageous sex.

sex : a love story

We need to realize that sex is a love story—not an ordinary love story, but an outrageous love story. An erotic love story. Outrageous love is Eros. Ordinary love is legitimate, but it is limited in the gift it can give you. In this world, that incarnation of the divine movement called outrageous love is the perpetual divine lovemaking. Participate in that perpetual movement of reality's lovemaking through your body and the result is not ordinary sex, but outrageous erotic sex. Enter into the inside of sex and you will find God, the sacred lover and gorgeous divine slut of the Cosmos. The inside of sex is outrageous love. The inside of sex is outrageous Eros. The qualities of Eros are the qualities of the sacred; the erotic and the holy are one. The goal is to re-eroticize all of your life, and your teacher and your guide is the sexual, the seat of all wisdom.

Each face of Eros is an expression of a different texture of radical aliveness. When all of these awaken in you, you are living an erotic life. Each face is a portal through which to return to Eros. The twelve faces are:

The First Face: Interiority: Living on the Inside
The Second Face: Fullness of Presence
The Third Face: Yearning and Desire
The Fourth Face: Wholeness and Interconnectivity
The Fifth Face: Uniqueness and Identity
The Sixth Face: Imagination
The Seventh Face: Perception
The Eighth Face: Giving and Receiving
The Ninth Face: Surrender
The Tenth Face: Play and Lishmah
The Eleventh Face: Creativity
The Twelfth Face: Pleasure and Delight

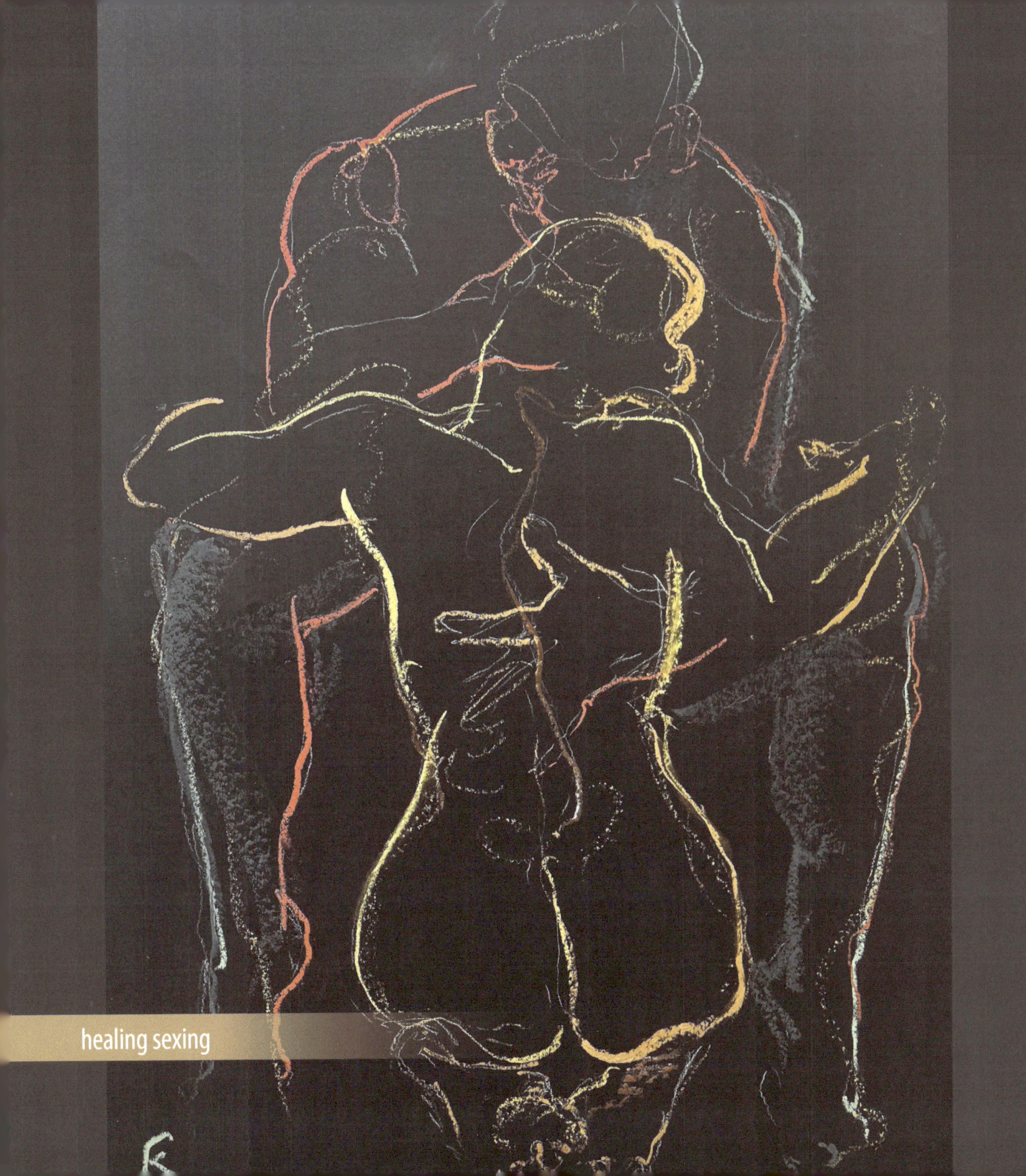

healing sexing

The experience of being radically alive comes from all of these faces of Eros taken together. To live the erotic life is to have the most potent and powerful access to each of these faces. In each of them, sex is our teacher. It is our portal to accessing the radically alive experience of each face. But our experience of the faces does not end in their sexual expression. Quite the opposite. It is all about sex and not about sex at all. Sex models each of the faces of Eros, and in so doing, gives us a vision of what it might mean to live them fully in every dimension of our lives.

It would be a great tragedy of the spirit if the only place where we experienced the faces of Eros were in the sexual. That would be to relegate Eros to the narrow confines of the bedroom, when it needs to soar through our kitchens, our offices, our carpools, our classrooms! In erotic living, we seek the realization of these qualities in every dimension of our existence. From work, to play, to politics, to intellectual pursuits—in all of these we seek erotic experience.

Erotic engagement could become our daily fare if we just freed our Eros from its old casing. These hand-me-down ideas of an Eros that is only about sex have become threadbare. We must reweave the fabric. The full pleasure of living, the joy of fullness and creativity, can come only when we re-eroticize our lives. Until then, human beings will turn to the shadows of Eros—rage, abuse, and violence—to remind themselves, through the intensity of those experiences, that they exist.

faces and paths

One of the fundamental principles of Eros is the path is the destination. In a true path, there is no split between the path and the goal. We are creative not only for the sake of the product that emerges but also for the sake of the creative experience itself. We do awareness practice not merely to get to awareness but also because the practice is awareness. We have sex, among other reasons, to feel intimate, but the experience of sex is intimacy itself. In the same way, the authentic and potent experience of each face of Eros is also the path to Eros.

The path and the destination are the same. Each face of Eros is a distinct path of Hebrew Tantra. In each, the sexual opens the door, giving us a taste of that particular face of Eros, so that Sex models for us each face of Eros so we can live that face in every dimension of our lives. The return to Eros cannot bypass sex because erotic sex models for us how to live erotically, how to be radically alive in all of the nonsexual dimensions of our lives.

The Secret of The Cherubs

reality is eros

Now that we understand that Eros lies at the heart of the temple mysteries, we can turn to the core question: If, as we have seen, the essence of the temple (and of every journey of spirit) is Eros, not sex, then why is sex such a prominent feature of the temple? This chapter will begin to unfold that information, which lies at the heart of the mystical Secret of the Cherubs.

The Secret of the Cherubs tells the story of the relationship between the erotic, love and the sexual. Sex models Eros. Erotic sex models what it means to be radically alive in every single facet of our lives. This is the new sexual narrative that is an affront to shame. The Secret of the Cherubs shows us the way to erotically reweave the very fabric of our lives in more vivid patterns, sensual textures, and brilliant hues. This is the path of what we have called Hebrew Tantra. Hebrew Tantra is both the invitation and the divine demand that we re-eroticize our lives.

The Secret of the Cherubs tells a new sexual story, one we have alluded to that now needs to be spelled out in its full erotic delight.

All great mysteries arise in response to powerful yet simple questions. If we were in a classroom, with the blackboards whitened with sketches of cherubs and notes on Eros, Shechinah, and sex, I would at this point step back and ask for questions, for all good spiritual maps should give rise to questions. Slowly a hand would be raised in the classroom… a second hand… a host of hands. The questions would begin: "If all that you have said so far is true, if Eros is not sex, then why in the temple of Eros is the centerpiece two sexually intertwined cherubs? Why sex? Why wouldn't the temple use some other image of Eros? Wouldn't a statue of a runner who has become the wind or a painter engrossed in his colors be a more fitting figure to perch atop the Ark? If Eros and love are, as you say, more than sex, then why does the temple insist on using a blatantly sexual image?" I would add a question of my own: "What is the magnetism of the cherubs and the Ark that has so fascinated the world for millennia?"

The Greek historian Thucydides reminds us that when words lose their meaning, culture collapses. A movie called Raiders of the Lost Ark goes blockbuster toward the end of the twentieth century. But why is the lost Ark so precious to us? Why are people so passionately committed—willing to risk it all—to recover the Ark? Why does the Ark have sexually entwined cherubs adorning its cover? These same cherubs appear in a sacred text in the book of Genesis guarding the entrance to the Garden of Eden. What precious secret do these cherubs hold in their embrace?

quest for the grail

Think of King Arthur and his valiant knights, who are all committed to the great quest for the Holy Grail. The grail is a goblet, in the mystery tradition, in the shape of the feminine yoni. In some Middle Eastern languages the very word for "grail," kos, connotes the wetness of the feminine yoni. The phrase "My cup runneth over" alludes to this hidden meaning in the mysteries of the grail. Arthur's knights of the round table are in devotion to the saving of the damsel in distress. For the grail tradition, this refers to the "redemption of the Shechinah"—the Goddess—which is the liberation of Eros. The table is round, a circle, alluding to the curves of the feminine. The popular The Da Vinci Code novel evokes the Mary Magdalene tradition, which sees Jesus and Mary in sexual embrace. Both the knights of Camelot and the Magdalene mysteries are sourced in the Secret of the Cherubs. Indeed, Jesus and Mary are no less than the cherubs above the Ark. The voice of God cannot be heard other than through their embrace. A church that denies Magdalene cannot hear the voice of God. Then, of course, there is the source of it all, Solomon, the great builder of the Jerusalem Temple, who marries a thousand wives. In the cherub tradition, the thousand wives symbolize the great erotic project of Solomon. The intention of his project was no less than the restoration of Eros to its proper position as the North Star of our lives.

Solomon, Wisdom of Solomon, Ark, lost Ark, grail quest, Temple in Jerusalem, Mary Magdalene, cherubs, damsel in distress, Da Vinci code—all of these are words that have lost their meaning in our culture. All of them are allusions to Eros. All of them have their source, in one form or another, in the Secret of the Cherubs, which lies at the epicenter of Solomon's temple. In recovering the meaning of the lost words, we both return to Eros and evoke the possibility of a new human and a new culture.

Contrary to the tenets of classical religion and much of psychology, Hebrew Tantra insists that sex is integrally related to love and Eros. Let's look again, one step deeper, at these three words and their relationship to one another. When we use the word love in this book, we mean what we referred to earlier as outrageous love. Outrageous love is the ceaseless inherent creativity of the cosmos that animates and seduces all of reality to ever higher and deeper emergence. Hebrew mystics teach that the universe in every second is always making love. The Kabbalists' word for it, zivug, connotes the outrageous erotic coupling that characterizes the cosmos at every level of reality. Outrageous love is Eros. Eros is love writ large, which is the essence of existence itself.

a new dimension of eros

Eros, as we have seen, is the experience of radical aliveness.

Now let's point to a new dimension to Eros. Inextricable from the erotic experience of radical aliveness is the powerful drive for union, the drive to make contact. One succinct definition of Eros therefore might be: Eros is radical aliveness passionately seeking contact. The drive for contact is, however, not merely an additional dimension of Eros. Radical aliveness is how the drive to contact feels.

Now let's add yet another dimension of Eros: Contact always births something new. New intimacy, new creativity, new emergence. We can now reformulate our definition of Eros. Eros is radical aliveness, passionately seeking contact, which always births something new. The erotic equation might be formulated as Eros = Radical Aliveness + Contact + Creativity.

Now we turn to sex. The sexual expresses the fundamental eroticism of all of reality, from the subatomic to the celestial to the human. But sex does not exhaust the eroticism of nature. The sexual is an expression of Eros; it is not the whole of Eros. Eros is the inner texture of reality that lives awake, alive, and aware in every moment. To wake up to Eros is to wake up to the shocking yet stunning realization that the universe is passionately making love all the way up and all the way down creation. Sex in the human realm is an expression of that same core yearning for contact—Eros—that drives all of reality. Sex is cosmic Eros performed in the flesh.

Cosmology tells us that we are made from stardust in constant equilibrium—attracted and held together by gravitational pull, kept apart by centrifugal force. We are partnered and yet separate—all part of the great cosmic Eros of reality.

four dimensions of the secret of the cherubs

Let's now state clearly the four major dimensions to the Secret of the Cherubs. The first dimension is that God is Eros. For the mystics, God is identical to reality, or life. To say that God is Eros is to say reality is Eros or life is Eros. The second dimension is that the sexual is an expression of the Erotic movement that characterizes every level of the cosmos. The third dimension is that the sexual in its ideal form models what it means to live radically alive and on purpose, in every other nonsexual dimension of life. Sex models Eros. It is in this precise sense that the sexual is the seat of all wisdom. The fourth dimension, central to the cherub mystics, is that conscious human sex actually transforms reality itself. Human sex does not only participate in the Eros of the cosmos; it is much larger than that. When human beings perform the cosmic Eros in their own flesh with the intention of tikkun—the healing and transformation of all that is—then, in the language of the mystics, a "great evolutionary fixing" takes place in all worlds above and below. For the cherub mystics, the miracle of life is not realized in some future world. The wonder of life is that we've met and been together in sexual union, making love here, "in this half-made world, where love is yet to take its hold."6 When we are together with the intention of restoring wholeness in a world of broken hearts, then we are living the erotic life.

Eros is the very aliveness of the cosmos expressed in all of its potency. When that potency awakens in you, your life becomes naturally good, true, and beautiful, and you become appropriately powerful beyond imagination. This is not a surface power that you wield against others, but a depth of power that allures others into the noble grace of your own full potency. When you awaken to the fullness of your own sexual power, you have the ability through your own erotic life to participate in the healing and transformation of all that is.

For the cherub mystics "the sexual union of man and woman" both models and participates in the more primal union of Shechinah (the divine feminine) and Tiferet (the divine masculine). By masculine and feminine, we do not mean man or woman but rather two essential forces of the universe. These universal cosmic forces are often referred to by the cherub mystics as lines and circles. They are different faces of the greater union, the force of divinity that courses through the cosmos and our own bodies. Their integration is the highest erotic expression of a healed world.

Now comes the truly radical insight! The human being is responsible for effecting the uniting of the masculine and the feminine in the God force. Entrusted to us is the sacred task of erotically merging the Shechinah and Tiferet, the Goddess and the God. We are the erotic mystics invested with the power to influence the force in powerful and profound ways.

This is possible because we reside in the undivided heart of God. It is not that we have power over God; rather, we have power as part of God. In our sexing we unite and balance the Shechinah and Tiferet poles within us. We heal the split in divinity. This is a sacred Tantric practice to unify, balance, and integrate the Shechinah and Tiferet, the circle and line poles within ourselves and in all of reality. We are bridge and balancer. It is we who bring home the exiled Shechinah. This erotic activism is modeled by the sexual but not exhausted by the sexual. That is what we mean when we say that sex models Eros. When we live the erotic life, in every dimension of our existence, then a tikkun, a "great evolutionary fixing," takes place in all worlds. The twelve faces of Eros, each modeled by the sexual—which we will unfold in the second half of this book—are the path to living the erotic life.

This fourth core dimension of the Secret of the Cherubs makes natural sense in light of contemporary science. Modern chaos theory grounds this activist principle in the material world in a phenomenon called "the butterfly effect." For example, the gentle breeze from a butterfly's wing on one side of the world can, two months later, be the "cause" of a windstorm on the other side of the world. If that is true about the effect of a butterfly, then imagine the impact of human beings consciously coupling—performing cosmic Eros in the flesh—with the intent of healing and transformation. For the cherub mystics, this kind of erotic activism is a core principle of human ethics.

Let's look more deeply at each of these dimensions. Eros is the fundamental movement in the universe toward contact. Sex is an expression of the core Eros of the cosmos. Sex is the drive for contact, the drive to bond, to connect, to be intimate. Sex is an expression of the drive to greater union, which is the creative essence of reality itself. In union, we all come home. But for the erotic mystics in the cherub tradition, home is not the boredom of perpetual rest but ground for ever greater and deeper union. Sex models the ecstatic urgency, which is the feeling of the drive to union.

In union, two separate parts do not fuse but rather make contact through intimate bonding to create newness. This newness is the greater union, the higher love, which is the yearning of reality's Eros. From quarks, to atoms, to molecules, to cells, to early organisms, to plants, to animals, to mammals, to ideas themselves, this core drive for contact is the Eros of all of reality.

Said differently, the great realization of the spiritually incorrect Tantric masters is that reality is allurement. Allurement is the quality of attraction, which is the very fabric of existence. From electromagnetic attraction to gravity to rungs of evolutionary emergence to the intellectual sex between ideas that generates newness—all of reality is moved by the intense allurement for contact, which generates new creations.

Way before sex appears on the scene, allurement is at work throughout the cosmos, attracting all expressions of creation to each other. From the first nanoseconds of the big bang to the first quarks that generated your body, to your own life, unique allurement is what drives all of life. Who are you if not your unique set of allurements? Your physical structure is the composite of the allurements that caused its atoms to form into molecules, its molecules into cells, and its cells into organs. Everything in creation is attracted to everything else, and this urge to know each other, to communicate, to join and make something greater, is the allurement that lies at the very heart of life.

Sex is an expression of this erotic drive. In human sex, Eros becomes conscious of itself. In conscious human sex, all levels of one's being are brought into higher union. This is the new sexual narrative that we have called sex erotic. Cosmic Eros is enacted in the flesh. Sex erotic transcends and includes the physical. The human being becomes the creative drive of the cosmos, all levels of body, mind, emotion, and spirit moving toward union. This is the core of the Secret of the Cherubs. We will go deeper into this truth about the nature of reality in our conversation about allurement, which is the third face of Eros.

hieros gamos

The esoteric term for the great love affair of the cosmos is Hieros Gamos. The Secret of the Cherubs is the primary source of this great mystical secret. Hieros Gamos is Latin for "the divine marriage." The divine marriage is the hidden mystical doctrine of the spiritually incorrect Tantric masters in virtually all of the great traditions. What does the divine marriage mean? It is not about God going shopping. Hieros Gamos is the hidden way of saying nothing less than "God is Eros." Or we might say even more directly, reality is Eros.

At every level of existence, two expressions of reality seek contact with each other to birth not only new but also higher and deeper orders of existence. These two forces used to be called masculine and feminine, but they are not gender specific. We can no longer exclusively identify them with men or women. They are two energetic qualities of the cosmos that live in all of reality, including in every human being. Borrowing a term from the erotic mystic Isaac Luria, we call these cosmic forces lines and circles. In Luria's evocative image, every moment of reality, on all levels and in all worlds, is born from the [unique] interpenetration of lines and circles that takes place in that moment. In other words, all of reality is erotic union.

Lines and circles were qualities of reality way before any gendered masculine and feminine existed. Line qualities include the forces of autonomy, independence, thrusting, and direction. In physics, these forces express as the particle (in contrast to the wave), centrifugal force, and the force of repulsion that opposes attraction. Circle qualities include the forces of allurement, attraction, reception, and cycle. In physics, these forces might be expressed as the wave (in contrast to the particle), centripetal force, and the quality of attraction that opposes repulsion. Physicist Niels Bohr insisted that a wave and a particle cannot exist separately from each other but are in a complementary both/and relationship, a sacred marriage of energy and matter.

The primary forces of lines and circles were already well known to the ancients. They are identified in the great traditions as God and Goddess or King and Queen. In Hinduism, they are called Shiva and Shakti,

In Taoism yin and yang. In Kabbalah, they are known by many terms, including Shechinah and Tiferet as well as the upper waters and the lower waters. In ancient Egypt, there were earth and sky. In the grail tradition, the knight with his linelike lance seeks the Holy Grail, the circlelike chalice. While these traditions often had markedly different visions of what constituted masculine and feminine, in all of them the goal is Hieros Gamos, some form of divine marriage in which the polarities are integrated into a larger whole. In science it was Niels Bohr who insisted that a wave and particle cannot exist separately from each other but in comple- mentary both/and relationship, a sacred marriage of energy and matter.

sex erotic

All of this forms the matrix of the new sexual narrative: sex erotic. Evolutionary theory, systems science, the new physics, the Kabbalistic Secret of the Cherubs, and the ancient knowing of Hieros Gamos all come together to weave this new sexual story. Reality is erotic. Human sexual Eros participates directly in the erotic nature of the cosmos. Or, said differently, human sexual eros models the great Eros of the cosmos at every level of reality. Reality is Eros, God is allurement, reality is allurement, the sexual models the erotic, God is Eros—all of these are potent expressions of the new sexual narrative for our time.

None of the classical sexual narratives—sex positive, sex negative, sex neutral, or sex sacred—have the capacity to address the fullness of our sexual experience. All are true, but only partially. Moreover, none of these four narratives is an affront to shame. It is only this fifth sexual narrative, sex erotic, the sexual story for our time, that has the potency to deconstruct shame. When you understand that at its source, sexual desire arises in you as the allurement of life itself yearning for contact, shame is eviscerated. The universe is erotic, motivated and animated by allurement and attraction. The sexual drive is but an expression of the core evolutionary Eros that moves all reality. It is only this spiritually incorrect but scientifically accurate understanding of reality that can birth a sexual narrative that honors the radical dignity of our desire.

from ethics to ethos

If you are with us up to this point, it will be self-evident to you that "reality is Eros" has absolutely nothing to do with inappropriate sexuality. Reality is Eros takes radical sexual ethics as a given. It addresses the next step beyond sexual ethics, upon which all sexual ethics depend. It is the articulation of a sexual ethos—that is to say, a sexual story that is true both to spirit and science and to our own deepest experience and yearning.

Reality as Eros is an ethos that speaks equally to liberal Protestants, progressive devout Catholics, Orthodox and liberal Jews, Southern Baptists, Colorado New Agers, singles, hipsters, Millennials, yuppies, and entrepreneurs of every color, nationality, creed, and orientation. Reality is Eros has nothing to do with whether you are monogamous, celibate, or polyamorous. It has nothing to do with your particular sexual style or code of behavior. The knowing that reality is Eros is, however, is core to your most fundamental vision of reality, and therefore your core experience of both your sexual and your erotic self. A complementary way of saying this is that God is Eros or God is love. Reality is love. Not ordinary love but outrageous love, the love that is Eros.

The reason that we add the words outrageous love—as we noted above—is because it has a power that the word love does not have by itself. Outrageous love is caring, compassionate, and kind. But outrageous love also has a fierce quality. This is the quality that the word outrageous connotes. In English, we do not have a word that captures the quality of reality that seamlessly arouses, attracts, allures, enchants, shatters, demands, and delights. We are so overwhelmed by the power of this quality that we assign to it a

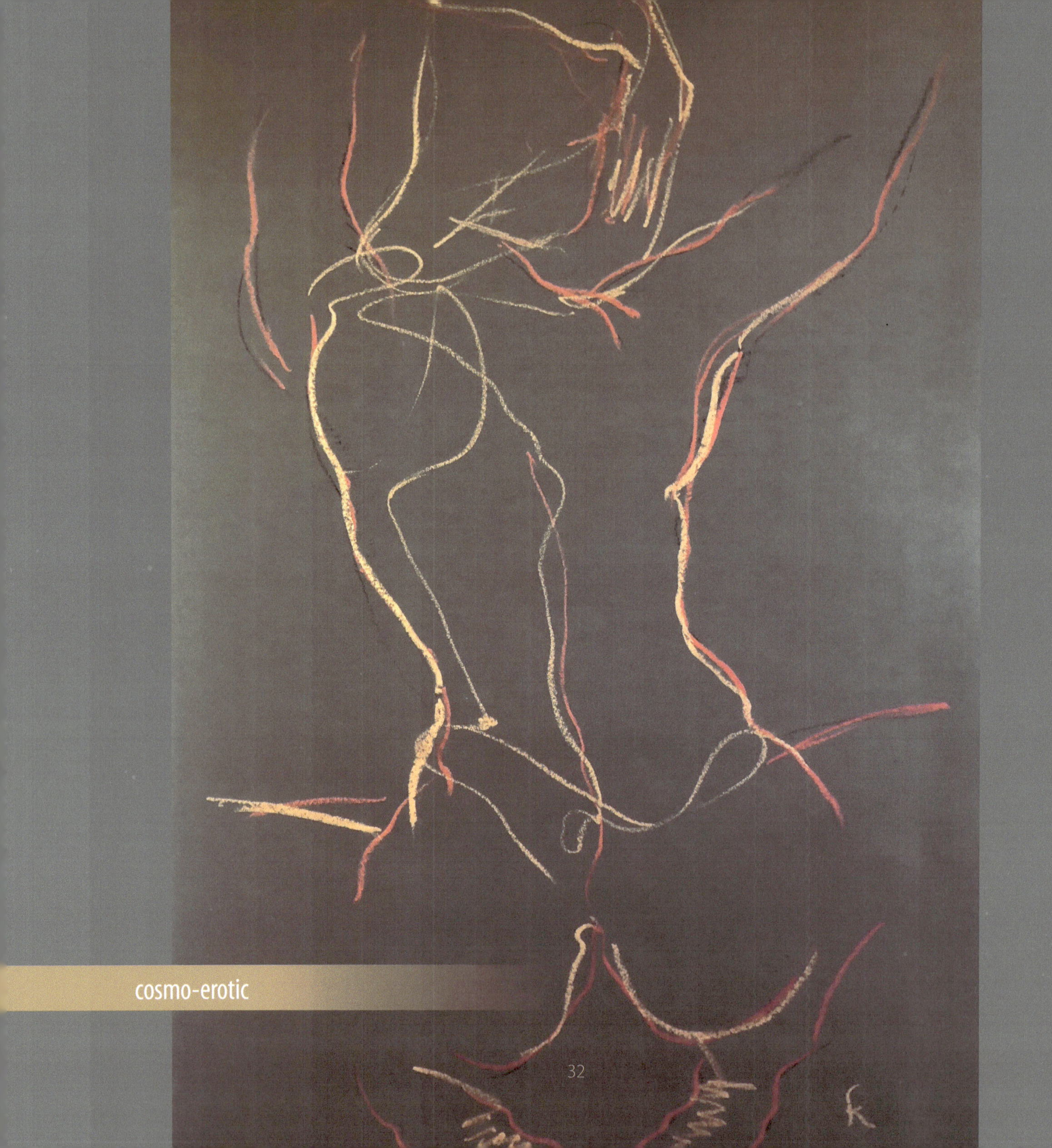
cosmo-erotic

word—outrageous—that is on the one hand confronting and demanding and on the other raw delight, desire, and amazement. Outrageous love is Eros.

Eros is not just sex. Sex is too small a word to contain the wholeness of Eros. Sex merely points toward Eros. Eros is so much greater. The erotic is the pulse of God beating at every level of reality. So, by Eros we do not mean human sex, but rather the cosmic Eros of which sex is but one potent expression.

If we trace sex to its source we realize that the body electric is plugged straight into God. Once you discover that current, you will never be the same.

loving the moment open

One of the principles that emerges from chaos theory contributes to a deeper understanding of the Secret of the Cherubs, and it is this: Every moment is either open or closed. Alfred North Whitehead, the great philosopher, reminds us that the "creative advance of novelty" is a defining feature of the cosmos. This means that reality opens to novelty in every moment. Or, as physicist Stuart Kauffman points out, we live in a ceaselessly creative universe. At the human level, the evolutionary impulse that drives the universe toward new depth moves us from unconscious growth to what evolutionary biologist Julian Huxley calls "conscious evo- lution." In Hebrew, the word development or evolution is the same word as opening. To evolve means to open. To awaken to conscious evolution is to come to realize that there is only one great human choice in every moment: to open or to close. The Secret of the Cherubs integrated with the leading edge of science informs us that the moment and the human being are not separate from each other. In every moment we have the choice to be open or closed. In other words, we have the choice to actually love open the moment—EVERY MOMENT—and the moment opens, or we can choose to remain closed, and the moment remains closed.

When we stay open in love we are pulsing alive in the flow of life. We then have the capacity to love the moment open. When the moment is opened, new life is created. If the moment remains closed, the potential new life is stillborn. It is therefore a simple evolutionary truth that to open or to close is no less than to love or to die. Those are the two evolutionary choices available in every moment.

creation every second

The reason that in every moment you must decide whether to be open or closed is because every moment is new. In every new moment you either love the moment open or you let the moment love you open. To love the moment open is to penetrate the moment. To be loved open by the moment is to let the moment penetrate you. That is what it means to be open and alive. The alternative is to be closed and dead.

The pivotal insight that every moment is a new quality of intimacy is core to the realization that reality is Eros. The erotic explosion in which the unmanifest becomes manifest is not a one-time event. Said differently, the big bang or creation did not happen once upon a time. It is—both mystically and scientifically—happening right now.

Eros is the initiating energy of the cosmos, the evolutionary impulse that creates all worlds; countless planets; myriad suns, moons, and stars; and every single particle of cosmic dust. Originally, creation, or the big bang, was thought to have been a one-time, initiatory event, an erotic divine implosion in which the primal line bisected the primal circle and the cosmos poured forth. Mystics and leading-edge quantum field theorists tell us differently. The erotic Hebrew mystic Levi Isaac opens his commentary with a radical assertion: creation is happening every second. The great flaring forth of reality is enacted anew every moment. As some quantum field theorists put it, reality flashes in and out of existence every moment. The very force of Eros, which is divinity, is constantly pouring through existence. God is Eros!

My (Kristina) eighth-grade science teacher, who was an avowed atheist, used to say, "You can't get something from nothing." He was only partially right, however. Within the atomic world, governed by the classic laws of physics, indeed, everything comes from something. But both the universe itself and the subatomic world—which contains the core building blocks of all of reality—literally come from nowhere. Reality is creatio ex nihilo—something from nothing.

In the language of the cherub mystics, we might say that reality was ecstatically exploded into existence by source. Creation is not from nothing but from no-thing. They call this yesh me-ayin. Yesh, "something," comes from ayin, which is best translated as "no-thing" or "the realm of pure possibility." But this erotic explosion that births reality is not a discrete event. The pulsing throb of outrageous love is the constant nature of reality, right now and now and now. Reality births new intimacy and new possibility in every moment.

All of reality as we know it is created out of subatomic particles. Quantum physics tells us that these particles flash in and out of the quantum field in every second. They are constantly popping in and out of existence. The particles pop out of our time, space, matter, energy, and the reality that we know into what is technically called a virtual state. This is a state of pure potentiality. It is in this sense that God is referred to by mystics as the possibility of possibility. Pure potentiality fiercely loves reality into existence in every moment. The two sexually intertwisted cherubs above the Ark in the Holy of Holies represent the constant movement of pure potentiality loving reality into existence anew in every second. This rhythm of reality is the core nature of all existence.

The brain operates in much the same way. Millions of separate signals throughout the brain are constantly flashing on and off. The place in the brain in which reality "disappears" before it turns back is in the synapses between neurons, the empty space that scientific language refers to as the gap between all neuronal connections. In the language of the cherub mystics, we might say that the gap is "the space between the cherubs." Mind the gap, for it is where creation mysteriously takes place.

According to neuroscience, there are some quadrillion synaptic connections that flash in and out of reality in the adult brain. It is in this gap that creation mysteriously takes place. Reality thus flashes in and out of existence through the perpetual Eros that emerges in the spaces in between. In the sacred texts of the Secret of the Cherubs, "the voice of God speaks from the space between the cherubs." The voice of God is no less than the constant ecstatic creativity birthed from pure potentiality, activated from synapses "in between."

What is so vital to realize is that this is not a one-time event but is the constant nature of existence.

In Hebrew, the implication of this perpetual Eros—the constant hidden intercourse of the cosmos—is captured in the word zeman. Zeman has three related meanings: "time," "invitation," and "radical readiness." The implication is that every moment in time is a new invitation. There is unrelenting optimism in this insight. The very depths of reality can be recreated in every moment. Yesterday can never define today. New possibility is constantly available. The pure potentiality of this moment births that which did not exist a moment ago. All trauma can therefore be healed. All pain can be transformed in the new moment.

What is required for that transformation is the third meaning of zeman: radical readiness. The image of a runner primed to sprint at the beginning of a race is helpful here. "Ready, set, go." It is that sense of being fully entered by the moment and fully penetrating the moment with your readiness that embodies the understanding that reality is zivug, reality is Eros. This is what St. Thomas knew when he said, "The dynamic pulse and throb of creation is the love of all things for the infinite." We might slightly reframe the end of the sentence to say, "the love of all things within the infinite." There is nothing apart from the infinite field of pure potentiality yearning to emerge. All of reality is penetrating and being penetrated all the way up and all the way down. All of reality is constantly making love with itself. This love awakens from hardwired instinct to human choice when we move from unconscious to conscious evolution.

Every moment waits for you to love it open. To love the moment open you must be fearlessly present, facing everything, avoiding nothing. In denial, the moment closes. In radical recognition coupled with audacious yet humble embrace, the moment opens. For the cherub mystics this is what it means to continuously make love with the divine one. This is what it means to live an erotic life, to be an outrageous lover. For the cherub mystics, the human being who awakens into full consciousness incarnates the throb and pulse of evolution.

The Cherub mystics understood that there is only one true choice we ever have, to open to close, to love the moment open or to close, and the moment stays closed. When we succumb to smallness, contraction, corruption, or unlove, the moment closes. When we expand into the full aliveness of our Unique Selves, we have the power to love the moment open and to receive the potent promise of that specific instant in time. When we talk about loving the moment open or letting the moment love us open, we are not talking about a sweet or even a gentle movement. We are talking about an intensity of presence, receptivity, and thrust that opens the moment to meet the implicit creative demand of its and our raw potency.

a sexual universe

We live in a sexual universe. From subatomic particles to the plant world, where the birds and bees are symbolic of the great pollination dance, to animals, plants, and humans, to the celestial attraction between planets, the fundamental structure of reality is allurement and attraction that creates profound contact at every level of the evolutionary chain. This is what we mean by Eros. We live in a universe driven by allurement. In that sense, we could say that reality is Eros all the way up to the highest spirit forms and all the way down to the smallest subatomic particles and the most essential forces of the universe.

a cosmos driven by eros

We live in a cosmos driven by Eros. The universe is a perfect, interconnected whole that at the same time seeks greater wholeness. The universe is radically alive, infused with presence and infinite vitality, even as it is infinitely intimate and whole. Everything rests in the being-ness of spacious perfection. And yet the universe is driven by evolutionary Eros. The cosmos is not only being but also becoming. Whereas being is characterized by harmony and equilibrium, becoming is characterized by a kind of ecstatic urgency and disequilibrium. Evolutionary Eros is constant becoming. It is the inherent, ceaseless desire for more and more contact and creativity. Consciousness yearns for contact. More contact always births new creativity. New creativity creates new babies of all kinds, or what science calls new evolutionary emergents. This is not an accident but the essential, sacred nature of an erotic universe. This is the lure of becoming that animates and drives all existence.

Walt Whitman caught a glimpse of this reality in his poem "Song of Myself":

Urge and urge and urge,
Always the procreant urge of the world.
Out of the dimness opposite equals advance,
always substance and increase, always sex,
Always a knit of identity, always distinction,
always a breed of life.

why sex is the ultimate model

The sexual models the erotic for two simple reasons. First, because reality is Eros. Second, because sex or allurement is the structural nature of reality, Eros all the way up and all the way down, it is utterly natural that the sexual models the erotic. It is almost self-evident that Eros should be the seat of all wisdom about reality. How could it be otherwise? Sex models the Eros of all reality, which inherently seeks more and more contact, mutuality, recognition, union, and embrace.

To paraphrase the evolutionary mystic Teilhard de Chardin, the fragments of the world, driven by the forces of Eros, seek each other so that the world may come into being. Desire is, at its most fundamental level, the desire for contact. Contact always births newness. The new thing might be a baby. Or it might mean a new level of intimacy. New might mean new creativity or possibility. In what evolutionary theorist Matt Ridley calls Idea Sex, "new" means new insight and new discovery that comes from intimate contact between ideas and people who are attracted to each other. Sex is an expression of the evolutionary Eros. The desire for contact is an expression of the core nature of the evolutionary Eros that drives all reality. This Eros animates every dimension of life. Sex models Eros means that sex is the arena where the ecstatic urgency of our drive to make contact is most apparent, most obviously pleasurable, and most self-evidently creative.

Eros

from fear to liberation

Eros—as we will see more clearly in the unfolding of the Secret of the Cherubs—is the core nature of reality, all the way up and all the way down the evolutionary ladder. When Eros awakens in us, it expresses itself as the radical drive for contact and connection. It is not a uniquely human impulse but rather the impulse of all of reality becoming conscious of itself in us. When we feel our Eros we feel radically alive and at home in the cosmos. We are filled with an unmistakable telos. We begin to live purpose-driven lives, which drip with the nectar of Eros itself. Our lives become telerotic.

eros is our birthright

Our bodies and hearts know that Eros is our birthright. It is not merely an intensifier of the ordinary. Rather, it points to the extraordinary energy at our core, which is the true marker of our deepest desire. The failure of Eros is the loss of aliveness that psychoanalyst Wilhelm Reich correctly diagnosed as the "emotional plague of man." It is not the loss of a particular privilege or experience. It is a deadening of all experience. The disconnection from Eros is cause for the loss of our unmediated knowing that life is good. When we become alienated from Eros, we forget our true identity and lose our dignity. We forget that we are good children of the universe that seeks our transformation. It is in the dignity of Eros that we recognize the glory of our true situation. It is in the dignity of Eros that we are personally addressed by reality. It is in the dignity of Eros that we know that we are needed, desired, and chosen by all that is.

bypassing eros creates abuse

The loss of the larger sense of Eros reduces Eros to mere sex. This, by its very nature, creates the rupture of contact and severing of connection that fosters the abuse of sex in all of its forms. Sex is abused when it is cut off from the larger context of Eros in which it lives. When sex is disconnected from the larger Eros, it cannot help but collapse on itself because we are asking far too much from it. Sex then implodes in every form of addiction and abuse. It is only when sex becomes a portal to the unique potency that flows through us from source—what we have called sex erotic—that the dignity and delight of Eros are restored.

When sex is cut off from our total being, from our deeper wholeness, and we ask it for favors it cannot grant, then Eros is degraded. It devolves from a blessing that bestows joy to an abusive curse that inflicts suffering. Abuse may appear as sexual harassment, rape, name rape, or false sexual complaints. Abuse results from the denial of our core equation, Reality = Eros. To deny Eros is to deny reality. Eros then reappears in degraded forms of sexual acting out or in the weaponizing of sex through false sexual stories. We must always remember that arousal is not consent and regret is not rape.

We must always stay connected to the goodness of Eros. Our disconnection from the aliveness of reality's inherent Eros results from our exiling of the larger Eros that animates all of reality into the constraints of merely sexual Eros. Sexual Eros comes alive when it begins to enact cosmic Eros. This is the narrative of sex erotic.

shame and guilt

Let's now revisit the principle that we introduced above. Shame is the root of all evil. Shame is different from guilt. Guilt is a healthy human emotion that arises when we have done something bad. Shame, by contrast, is the experience not that we have done something bad but that we are bad. Shame is the feeling that we are somehow broken and cannot be fixed. More often than not, shame is rooted in something sexual. Self-images of control, artificial dignity, status, appropriateness, and more all need to be surrendered at the altar of the sexual.

Because the sexual challenges our conventional sense of identity, to heal shame we must articulate the new sexual narrative of sex erotic. In sex erotic, the sexual models the erotic. It is paradoxically the greater Eros that illuminates and eroticizes the small eros. Shame is when sex stops short of infinity. We heal shame when we realize that the sexual does not regress our identity but rather it expands and evolves our identity. The sexual, as we will show when we discuss the twelve faces of Eros, offers us a glimpse into who we might be if we realized who we already are.

the universe feels

The universe feels, and the universe feels the pulse and throb of Eros. It feels the intensity of desire and passion that is expressed in the word ***erotic***. The greatest human desire is to participate in the Eros of reality. But we are afraid of the feeling of the erotic. It makes us feel out of control or vulnerable in a way we would rather deny or repress. It is only by entering the pounding surge of Eros and tracing it back to its original divine source that we begin to live the erotic life. But if we bypass the pounding surge it will demand its pound of flesh. The feeling of erotic desire is the incessant longing of the universe to meet other forms of itself in order to birth new creations from the joy of that contact.

recovering our memory of zivug

The great zivug of the cosmos has been forgotten. We forget that we live in a reality whose core principle is allurement. For the Greeks, the loss of knowledge is the source of all evil. For the erotic mystic, the loss of memory is the source of all evil. Our failed memory of zivug is the source of great pain and confusion. On the one hand we forget that, according to the leading edge of quantum theory, reality is coming in and out of existence in every second. Mystics call the interior of this same phenomenon "constant creation." Constant creation is the outrageous love, what the mystics call zivug matmedet—perpetual Eros—which fiercely and tenderly loves reality into being in every second.

However, it is not only that we have forgotten. In addition, our denial of the erotic is so desperate and intense that we have forgotten that we have forgotten. And yet, in the midst of our amnesia, we yearn to participate in the Eros of the cosmos. Anything less will not satisfy us. We yearn for what we have forgotten, and so we cannot explain our yearning to ourselves. We no longer understand our innermost drives. We have lost touch with the radical yearning for intense contact that is the axiomatic desire of reality alive in us.

fear of eros

Why are we so afraid of Eros? The erotic, at its core, is the primal drive to make contact. It is the urge to merge—at least temporarily—with another being. It is an urge that is so intense that we are willing to give up much of our vaunted sense of dignity and self to accomplish it. But we are afraid of this urge because it undermines our sense of identity. The illusion of being a self-sufficient, separate being, independent and autonomous, is significantly challenged or shattered by Eros. We assume that this undermining of identity is regressive. Therefore, we fight it—personally, religiously, and culturally—with everything we have, because identity is the lifeboat we desperately need to feel safe in the world.

But what if the undermining of identity catalyzed by the erotic was not regressive but expansive and evolutionary? What if we really understood that Eros is the stirring within the infinite awakening as our arousal? What if erotic desire in all of its expressions simply reminded us that we are interconnected—that we need each other? What if the beds of our delight invited us to the practice of our devotions? That is what we mean when we say that sex models Eros.

This is the hidden Tantric teaching of non-rejection that appears in every great tradition. In Hebrew Tantra—the Secret of the Cherubs—we enter desire and trace it to its root, the ceaseless creativity of the cosmos that is perpetually birthed through ever more intimate contact. Desire is the doorway into the elemental Eros and allurement that drives all of reality. Desire models the great yearning for connection and contact.

Because we can't see that Eros is a doorway, we make it into a closed room with no way in or out. We then proceed to identify the erotic with its most degraded forms, hence our intense and even desperate fear of the erotic.

The Secret of the Cherubs is simple: we degrade Eros because it makes us feel out of control, but hidden in the erotic is the very source code of the cosmos itself. Reality itself is Eros. Awakening to our sexual longing models our desire to live a fully erotic life in every dimension of existence. The Secret of the Cherubs is that the great Eros of the cosmos is hidden in the small eros of sex.

Since reality is Eros—one core expression of which is pleasure—a vacuum of Eros or pleasure is intolerable. So the child begins to fill himself with what might be called "negative pleasures." Both the term and the idea are rooted in key passages in Freud's writing. When you lose contact with the larger erotic life force, you turn away from life. You take the energy of pleasure back into yourself, where it twists and distorts. It appears as withholding, anger, resentment, and inappropriate aggression. The natural erotic current of "yes" energy is turned into "no." The child defines herself by protecting her separate self from all that is outside of her boundary. At the same time, her natural allurement to Eros and pleasure is disowned and goes underground.

Materialist psychology tries to subdue Eros and pleasure by identifying it with personality dysfunction or neurosis. But pleasure is not an aberration from reality. At its core, the pleasure principle is the reality principle. The rupture of our experience from Eros and pleasure is therefore a primal alienation from reality itself.

Denial, as psychology has well documented, always demands its proverbial pound of flesh. Denial of our essential erotic nature will always create distortion of the most tragic kind. As social philosopher Norman O. Brown writes in explanation of Freud, when taken too far, the alienation from Eros is the path of sickness and self-destruction. The repression of libido turns the lack of Eros into pain.

Wilhelm Reich calls this alienation from Eros the emotional plague of man. When man's erotic force is blocked, it turns in on itself, seeking expression. The result, he says, is that "man can murder, rape, and pillage." Reich was perhaps Freud's most brilliant student. Reich broke with Freud over the latter's inability to understand the cosmic nature of Eros. The hidden fear of the full power of Eros remains with us throughout our lives, expressing itself in many ways. One way the fear manifests is in our relationship with pleasure. Whenever we go to engage pleasure, the original "no" of culture or parents shows up. That first "no" was sharp and painful. We experienced it not as a "no" to something external to us but as a "no" to our essential selves. Our core desire, our most primal "yes," was rejected. The pain of that originally rejected Eros is reawakened every time we move toward Eros or pleasure. The original fear of Eros, learned in our earliest years, is layered with the pain of rejection that our original erotic "yes" occasioned. The fear of Eros is thus a kind of double loop that shapes our entire lives.

Fear of Eros fosters the alienation that lies at the heart of our culture. Freud is a primary example of this disconnection from Eros that has contributed so much to our modern disease. Freud identified the pleasure principle as being characteristic of the earliest stages of life before a child matures. At maturity, he argued, the reality principle supplants the pleasure principle: the ego then guides the id as the child's new North Star. Should the pleasure principle reappear inappropriately in the child's life, that is considered "regressive." But this Freudian philosophy sets up pleasure and Eros in opposition to reality. In fact the opposite is true: Eros is the very nature of reality all the way up and all the way down the chain of being. To set up a semantic field in which pleasure and reality are antonyms is a potent expression of our fear of Eros. To return to Eros, we must therefore establish the core principle of reality as Eros.

THE FIRST FACE

1

interiority : living on the inside

The first face of EROS is to be on the inside. Whether it's the inside of a text, whether it's the inside of a relationship, whether it's the inside of a conversation. There's this place where you break through to the inside.

The esoteric Hebrew term for the Holy of Holies is Lifnai Lifnim. Literally rendered into English, this means "the inside of the inside." In another architectural expression of this idea, the temples of the Masonic Order have doors that open only from the inside. The Hebrew word for "inside" is panim, but it has other meanings as well.

There is a third meaning to the Hebrew word panim. In a slightly modified form, it means "before," in the sense of appearing before God. For the Erotic mystics of the Solomon lineage rooted as they are in the magic and spells of language, it is an entirely different affair. Once the journey to God is finished, the infinite journey in God begins.

Being on the inside is not about a geographical place, but about a soul terrain, a place inside ourselves. Socrates writes at the end of the Phaedrus, "Beloved Pan and all ye other gods that haunt this place, give me beauty in the inward soul, and may the inward and outward man be at one."

For the temple mystics, exile occurs when one's inside and outside are not connected in day-to-day living. Exile is non-erotic living. When I am not living from the inside, I am not living naturally. My choices, reactions and responses do not emerge spontaneously from my interior castle.

Interiority is the experience of being and feeling like we are on the inside—on the inside of life, the inside of where it's all happening, the inside of Love, the inside of Eros.

interiority

the sexual models the erotic:

"Being on the inside" means not on the inside of your sexual partner, for that is limited to the masculine sexual experience. Rather it is about being on the inside of the experience itself. Sex models Eros because in great sex you enter the inside of the inside. In great sex time stands still, concerns of the exterior world fall away as we enter into the secret garden. The external gives to the eternal.

Novelist Roman Payne give visceral expression to the experience of entering the inside through the sexual body.

"When I touched her body,
I believed she was God.
In the curves of her form
I found the birth of Man,
the creation of the world,
and the origin of all life."

Sex is a portal to being on the inside. Sex models Eros however it does not exhaust Eros. Being on the inside is not limited to sex. It is modeled by sex. Sex reminds us that we long for the inside places.

Sufi poet Rumi puts it this way:

The real orchards and fruits are inside the heart;
the reflection of their beauty is falling upon this water and earth.
All the deceived ones come to gaze on this reflection
in the opinion that this is the place of paradise.

They are fleeing from the origins of the orchards; they are making merry over a phantom.

What Rumi is saying is that the eros of beauty dwells within us. All the exterior beauty in the world is just a reflection of that. People who do not understand Eros think paradise can be attained by immersing themselves in the beauty of external objects. But in chasing material pleasures for their own sake, they actually turn away from the source of those pleasures, which is the eros within. They pursue a phantom, an echo of Eros, instead of Eros itself. They are on the outside, exiled from Eros. Those who know "the real orchards and fruits are inside the heart" are on the inside, intimate with Eros.

All that we hold most important in life is an interior. Values and meaning are interiors. Love, loyalty, and beauty are all interiors. To live an erotic life, we need to be in touch with the inside. The return to Eros begins with the return to the inside.

The key point is that the sexual takes us inside to a place of potent interior knowing, both about our core identity and our place in the universe. The sexual takes us inside and changes our interior knowing. That is what we mean when we say the sexual models the erotic. But it is even more than that. Sex becomes not only a model but also a method to catalyze potent breakthrough it the most pivotal arenas of our nonsexual lives.

THE SECOND FACE

fullness of presence

The Shechinah in the temple is termed "the indwelling presence." The erotic is always the experience of full presence. The Shechinah, say the mystics, is waiting for us to show up.

The Shechinah is presence waiting for us to be present. She is Eros, standing outside our window, waiting. Waiting for us to feel her presence. Waiting for us to be overwhelmed by her love. Waiting for us to run out and behold with wonder… her face.

Fullness of presence is not a quality that is distinct and different from the erotic quality of being on the inside. Presence flows naturally with, and even overlaps, interiority. And yet it is not quite the same. Of course, being on the inside requires the fullness of presence. Presence is about showing up. Presence means I am fully showing up right here. I am not anywhere else in this moment.

The Sexual Models the Erotic: It is in the sexual where – in its ideal expression – we are most fully present to each other. It is in the sexual that we most fully show up. In the sexual we both give and receive rapt attention. Every gesture, fragrance, sigh, and whisper ripples through us as we listen deeply to the erotic instructions that well up from the depth of our soul's body.

Sex models Eros because in great sex your experience a radical fullness of presence. Adrienne Rich, who brought lesbian sexuality into the forefront of poetic discourse, captures the sense of radical presence in the sexual:

> *Whatever happens with us, your body*
> *will haunt mine - tender, delicate*

fullness of presence

In the fullness of presence, the Eros lives in memory with such clarity that it continues to arouse even decades later.

your lovemaking…
the live, insatiate dance of your nipples in my mouth —
Presence never disappears:
your touch on me, firm, protective, searching me out, your strong tongue and slender fingers reaching

When we are touched by true erotic arousal the quivering tenderness feels forever. The erotic poetess than takes us home

where I had been waiting years for you
in my rose-wet cave – whatever happens, this is

Eros is about feeling the fullness of being, the opposite of emptiness. Life is what you do with your emptiness. The way to approach emptiness is not try to fill it but simply to be mindful of it. To notice the emptiness. Only when we can hold the emptiness does it become filled with the divine voice.

The path to Eros is filled with detours to pseudo Eros, but they are all dead ends. When we are so desperate for fullness, when the emptiness hurts too much, these detours seduce us off the path, often spinning us to painful places we never wanted to go.

Life is about walking through the void. Every time we walk through and not around the void, we come out stronger. Every time we are seduced by pseudo Eros, ethical breakdown is around the corner. There is no ethics without Eros.

THE THIRD FACE

yearning and desire

When I am on the inside, when I am fully present, I am able to access the third face of the erotic experience—yearning. Yearning, or desire, is an essential expression of love and Eros. As long as I am on the outside, I can ignore my deepest desires and stifle my longing. But longing is a vital strand in the textured fabric of Eros. It is of the essence of the Holy of Holies.

You see, I want a lot,
Perhaps I want everything:
the darkness that comes with every infinite fall
And the shivering blaze of every step up.
So many live on and want nothing,
and are raised to the rank of prince
by the slippery ease of their light judgements.
But what you love to see are faces
That do work and feel thirst.
- Rainer Maria Rilke

Eros is to be on the inside, including the inside of your desire. Being on the inside invites you to clarify your desires, yet not transcend them. True desire is attained through the deep meditation in which you access the internal witness. This is a place of detachment, from which you survey with penetrating but loving eyes all of your desires. This place of internal witness allows you to move beyond an addictive attachment to any particular desire. At that point the person engaged in ***birur*** (clarification) does not abandon desire. Rather, she moves to connect with those desires that are truest to her deepest and most authentic self. It is, as T. S. Eliot once wrote, in the empty space "between the spasm and the desire" that the person is born.

For the Erotic mystic of the Solomon lineage, detachment is a strategy, not a goal. In the end, you must not remain a spectator in the drama of your own existence. Rather, you need to become the lead actor on your stage by always living on the inside and never getting lost in the luxury of distance or detachment, so you can fully merge with the part the universe has invited you to play. Longing and desire are good not because we believe that all of our yearning will be fulfilled or realized, but because the yearning itself fulfills us. The desire itself fills the emptiness. When we yearn to grow, when we are alive with desire, we touch fulfillment.

the sexual models the erotic:

The yearning for contact is of the essence of the sexual. Indeed, the yearning is often thought by poets and psychologists to be more pleasurable and intense than the fulfillment itself. Another word for yearning or longing is desire. Sex and desire are so inextricably bound that the very word desire evokes the sexual.

The sexual models the erotic. Yearning models the desire of reality itself to evolve towards more and more creativity, love, complexity and consciousness. Yearning is the interior feeling of evolution.

Sex models Eros because in great sex you experience the yearning force of being. Sex models Eros because the same desire that drives us to make sexual contact drives all of reality to make erotic contact. It is precisely this erotic contact at every level of reality –from electromagnetic to cellular to cultural – that drives all of reality.

In living the Erotic life, you feel the yearning- the radical desire- for more and more complexity, consciousness, creativity, love, and uniqueness. At the most essential level reality is desire. It is in the sexual that we are meant to access both the dignity and demand of desire.

yearning and desire

THE FOURTH FACE

wholeness and interconnectivity

on the intimate universe, reality as allurement

Longing, desire, and tears remind us of the fourth strand in the erotic weave. They whisper to us that we are all interconnected within a greater wholeness. No life stands alone. Reality is a larger whole in which all is interconnected. Everything is connected to everything else. Everything yearns for ever deeper contact. We are all parts of a larger whole.

This is what the ancient mystics meant when they said in the book of Genesis, "It is not good for the human to be alone." The word good is the key refrain in chapter one of Genesis. After every stage of the world's emergence, the text reads, "God saw that it was good." Then in chapter two, the text suddenly exclaims, "Lo tov heyot ha'adam levado" ("It is not good for the human to be alone"—or better translated from the Hebrew, "to be lonely"). All of the good of creation is "not good" if we are lonely. To be lonely is not merely a human neurotic condition—it is in violation of the essential nature of life, which is interconnected and whole. To be lonely is to be cut off from the interior of another, isolated in surface existence. Living on the outside, by yourself, is nonerotic, no matter how successful you are or how many people you are surrounded by.

To be lonely is to be apart and not a part of. The truth is that everything is part of the great whole. The world is not in a natural state of war but in a natural state of Eros. Everything is fundamentally interconnected. No part is apart from the larger wholeness. All parts are an inex- tricable part of the whole. Indeed, the very fabric of reality is parts and wholes. Every part is both a whole unto itself and part of a larger reality. This is the nature of existence all the way up and all the way down the chain of being. Nothing stands

wholeness and interconnectivity

apart. All is interconnected as part of the great whole of the universe.

Eros is what allows us to move past the feeling of isolation and separation and experience ourselves as part of the quilt. To sunder our connection to Eros is therefore to sin. Not only would we lose the source of life's greatest pleasure, but we would also undermine the building blocks of connection without which the world would ultimately collapse.

an intimate universe

The interwoven universe is the interconnected universe. Interconnectivity takes place in wholeness, the fourth face of Eros. Interconnectivity is the exterior face of wholeness. The interior of wholeness is intimacy. Or, said differently, the interior of interconnectivity is intimacy.

Eros makes one grand proclamation about the nature of reality. We live in an intimate universe. That is what we mean when we say that reality is Eros. Existence is interconnection, and that means that the universe feels. The universe feels intimate. To be non-intimate is to be out of integrity, for integrity means to be integrated, to be connected with, to be interwoven in the larger fabric of being. We might say that intimacy is integral. Anything that is not integral is not intimate, or not erotic. Integral means that the parts are connected and intimate with each other.

the sexual models the erotic :

Wholeness and Interconnectivity is nowhere more clearly manifested than in the sexual drive. We are born with an urge to merge. We do not feel whole unto ourselves. We feel like we are part of a larger whole. The sexual never lets us forget that we are not whole merely unto ourselves. The sexual reminds us constantly that we yearn for connection and wholeness beyond our separate selves. In great sex you feel the urge to connect, to make the deepest possible contact, to be the most intimate that you can possibly be. In that contact, in that connection, in that intimacy you become more whole. Pablo Neruda is direct in his understated declaration of this drive for connection that animates all of reality.

I want to do with you what spring does with the cherry trees. - Pablo Neruda

Sex models Eros because the drive for connection, for great wholeness, that moves the sexual is the same drive for wholeness and connectivity that motivates all of our social, cultural and creative endeavors.

But the sexual model of the erotic in this face of interconnectivity and wholeness is even more fundamental than that. For classical mystics like Plato, sex models Eros because in the sexual we are drawn to merge with the prior unity, the original wholeness that inexorably calls us home. For the evolutionary cherub mystics, sex models Eros because the experience of Wholeness promised by the sexual is the strange attractor which allures the entire evolutionary process forward.

« We long to return to Eros. That means we want to live erotically in all the dimensions of our life."

We live in a cosmo-erotic universe. The universe is driven by evolutionary Eros, the desire for contact in order to form ever deeper and ever greater wholes.

THE FIFTH FACE

uniqueness and identity

the erotics of uniqueness and identity

The Eros of oneness, of non-separation—in which all are interconnected as part of the great whole—that is just part of the story. We are also, wonderfully and radically unique. Each person is an individual, different from every other. And our uniqueness is not an accident of nature that should be overcome. It is not a property of the ego to be transcended. Uniqueness is a quality of Eros and essence. Uniqueness is erotic. We are not merely True Self or what we sometimes call cosmic self. We are also Unique Self. Only the experience of our radical uniqueness can truly fulfill us. Only the realization that we are Unique Selves opens the door to living the erotic life. Living our Unique Self is an essential portal in our return to Eros. Eros is rooted in personal identity. When our core identity collapses, our Eros fails, and we fall out of the erotic life.

Your identity is not a complex equation. It is rather the direct answer to the great question that must guide every life. That question is: Who are you? The answer is that you are both a True Self and a Unique Self. There is no True Self without Unique Self. By True Self we mean your essential consciousness, which is indivisible from the larger field of consciousness. Your True Self is the singular that has no plural. The total number of True Selves in the world is one. Your True Self, however, has an irreducibly unique perspective and an irreducibly unique quality of intimacy. It can be expressed in the following equation:

True Self + Unique Perspective + Unique Quality of Intimacy = Unique

Self As a person, you are not merely True Self (sometimes called No Self) as the great Eastern traditions claimed. You are also an irreducibly unique expression of the love intelligence and love beauty of all that is. The love intelligence and love beauty that drives all reality lives in you, as you, and through you. There is no one like you that ever was, is, or will be. You are your True Self, and you are also your gorgeous and irreplaceable Unique Self.* It took existence nearly fourteen billion years of complex and dazzlingly precise synchronicities to produce you. Your cellular signature is the unique dance of seventy-five trillion unique cells—unlike any others that ever were, are, or will be—in unique symphonic relationship.

sex is personal

When we have great sex the personal and unique are at the center of the experience. In that sense sex is the ultimate form of relationship between two unique selves.

I hunt for a sign of you in all the others,
In the rapid undulant river of women,
Braids, shyly sinking eyes,

Light step that slices, sailing through the foam.

Suddenly I think I can make out your nails,
Oblong, quick, nieces of a cherry:
Then it's your hair that passes by, and I think
I see your image, a bonfire, burning in the water.
I searched, but no one else had your rhythms,
Your light, the shady day
you brought from the forest;
Nobody had your tiny ears.
You are whole, exact,
and everything you are is one,
And so I go along, with you I float along, loving
A wide Mississippi toward a feminine sea.
- Pablo Neruda

Sex models Eros: because the sex is both radically unique and personal even as it is radically impersonal. In sex we are all unique and in sex we are all the same.

sex is impersonal :

At the same time, the sexual impulse that arises in us is an expression of the seemingly impersonal evolutionary Eros of all of reality, incessantly driving all of reality- us included- to more and more contact, creativity and aliveness. Sex is deeply personal and deeply impersonal. Sex like of all of our erotic lives, is both radically personal and impersonal. We are simultaneously all unique and all the same.

We connect through our uniqueness –our puzzle piece nature that connects us to the larger puzzle and we connect through our sameness –we are all part of the same puzzle. In this precise fashion the sexual models the fifth face of Eros, our simultaneous sameness and uniqueness.

unique self = yoni + phallus

Reality is Eros, has nothing to do with inappropriate sexuality. It has everything to do with loving the moment open and being loved open by the moment. To love the moment open, and be loved open by the moment requires the erotic energies of both yoni and phallus that live in each of us. To love the moment open is to penetrate so deeply into the Eros of the moment that something new and sacred is born.

'who are you ?'

You are reality's eyes, hands, feet and love. You are a unique expression of evolution. You are here to write the poem that only you can write. You are here to sing the song that only you can sing. You are here to be the unique presence of being and becoming in the world that no one else but you can be.

Your deepest desire and greatest pleasure as a human being is to become transparent to the interior faces of the cosmos yearning to evolve through you. The yearning of the cosmos to evolve shows up as the evolutionary impulse

uniqueness and indentity

living in you. Your unique self, your unique allurements, are the personal face of the evolutionary impulse—awakening in you, as you, and through you. When you awaken to your unique self, and you invite the yearning of the cosmos to singularly fulfill itself through your eyes and your heart and your hands, you are living the erotic Life.

the four erotic truths

To fully embrace your beautiful, unique self, you need to realize four erotic truths:

1) Your uniqueness means that you are intended by reality.
2) Your uniqueness means that you are chosen by reality.
3) Your uniqueness means that you are loved.
4) Your uniqueness means you are needed by reality.

We are each leading men and women in the great play of cosmic Eros. The polish poet, Nobel laureate, Wislawa Szymborska, writes about coming to grips with this sense of the utter necessity of our roles in the great cosmic drama.

I know nothing of the role I play.
I only know it's mine. I can't exchange it...
You'd be wrong to think that it's just a slapdash
quiz taken in makeshift accommodations. Oh no.
I'm standing on the set and I see how strong it is.
The props are surprisingly precise.
The machine rotating the stage has been
around even longer.
The farthest galaxies have been turned on.
Oh no, there's no question,
this must be the premiere.
And whatever I do will become forever
what I've done.

To live your story is to be able to hear the intimate whisper of divinity erotically caressing your life. We are all recipients of cosmic love notes.

The artist inside us is "all the time on the lookout for material to make a dream with... inspiration means being able to take the hint... It is not only a tuned responsiveness; it is also an unconscious radar for affinities, for what speaks to one by calling up one's own voice."

-Adam Phillips

the storying of sex

the connection between sex and story is hardwired into our spiritual operating system, so much so that we have a universal name for one who separates his or her personal story from the sexual. We call that person a prostitute. The essence of the prostitute archetype in every culture is the de-storying of the sexual.

When the divine Shechina Goddess achieves union with the divine male God, it is called kissing. The human and the Divine mirror each other in Kabbalistic myth.

When there is no kissing, the Shechina is in exile. She is Eros exiled into the merely sexual. She is Shechina degraded to being a prostitute.

A Fifth-Face Story

the harlot by the sea

The themes of the previous chapters on voice and unique self, come into sharp focus in a fabulous but little-known myth told by the third century Babylonian wisdom masters.

Once there was a man who was very careful in his fulfillment of the law of ritual fringes. Ritual fringes are items of clothing recommended by the Torah to help preserve purity. This man heard about a certain harlot by the sea who accepted four hundred gold coins as her wage. He sent her four hundred gold coins and fixed a time for their encounter. When the day arrived, he came and waited at her entrance. Her maid came and told her, "That man who sent you four hundred gold coins is here and waiting at your door." To which she replied, "Let him enter." When he came in, she prepared for him seven beds, six of silver and one of gold, and between one bed and the other there were steps of silver, but the last steps were of gold. She went up to the top bed and lay down on it naked. He also went up after her to sit naked, facing her.

At that very moment, his ritual fringes ascended the stairs by themselves and slapped him in the face, whereupon he slipped off the bed and sat on the ground. She also slipped off and sat on the ground. She swore, "I will not leave you alone until you tell me what blemish you saw in me."

He swore, "Never have I seen a woman as beautiful as you. But there is a commandment called `ritual fringes,' and the ritual fringes have appeared to me. They represent to me a higher order of value. I cannot sleep with you."

She said, "I will not leave you until you tell me your name, the name of your village, the name of your teacher, and the name of the academy in which you study Torah." He wrote it all down and placed it in her hand. She then arose and divided her wealth in three parts. A third she used

harlot by the sea

to pay taxes, a third she gave to the poor, and a third she retained. However, the beautiful bedsheets she had used on her harlot's bed she kept with her.

She then came to the study hall of Master Hiyya (the man's teacher). "Give me instructions," she said, "so that I may convert."

"My daughter," replied the master, "perhaps you have set your eyes upon one of my students." (In which case her desire to convert may have been insincere and thus legally invalid.)

She took out the paper on which the man had written his name and the name of his village, master, and school. Upon seeing the note, R. Hiyya agreed to convert her. "Go," he said, "and enjoy your acquisition. [You may marry him.]"

The very sheets she spread for the man as a harlot she now spread for him as his wife.

But who is she, our harlot woman? At this point, she is an archetype. She is the sexual incarnate. Relationship, depth, and commitment are not her trade. She deals in fantasy, filling up men's emptiness with peak experiences that crash the next morning. In the image of the Zohar, she is the Shechina in exile, the lost princess.

"I will not leave you alone until you tell me what blemish you saw in me."

Your identity is not a complex equation. It is rather the direct answer to the great question which must guide every life. That question is: Who are you?

...the wondrous experience of being seen. To be seen is to be loved. Love is perception.

THE SIXTH FACE

imagination

homo imaginus

French philosopher Gaston Bachelard was right when he wrote of imagination, "More than any other power it is what distinguishes the human psyche."Or listen to Norman O. Brown, the twentieth-century prophet of Eros: "Man makes himself, his own body, in the symbolic freedom of the imagination. The eternal body of man is the imagination." We turn to the Erotic mystical master of the Solomon lineage, Nachman of Bratslav: "It is for this reason that man was called Adam: He is formed of adamah, the dust of the physical, yet he can ascend above the material world through the use of his imagination and reach the level of prophecy. The Hebrew word for 'I will imagine' is adameh."

Man emerges from nature to live "a fantasy-aroused existence."

Imagination is neither a detail of our lives nor merely a methodological tool. It is the very essence of who we are. We generally regard ourselves as thinking animals, Homo sapiens. French philosopher René Descartes' "I think, therefore I am" is hardwired into our cultural genes. The erotic mystics articulated a far more resonant sense of the nature of our humanity. The closest Hebrew word to "human," or the Latin homo, is adam. The word adam derives from the Hebrew root meaning "imagination" (de'mayon). The stunning implication is that the human being is not primarily Homo sapiens but what we will call Homo imaginus.

Man is described as being created in the divine image. "Divine image" does not mean a fixed and idolatrous copy of divinity. God has no fixed form. Instead, God is the possibility of possibility. We saw how the biblical opposition to graven images was grounded in the refusal to limit God to the confines of an image. Consequently, the statement that human beings were created in the divine image should be understood in two ways. First, humankind is not so much "made in God's image" as we are "made in God's imagination"—we are a product of the divine fantasy. Second, human beings actually participate in the divine imagination—we are Homo imaginus.

How different this understanding is from the bleak depression of modern existential thinking! Our longing for the good is dismissed by existentialist philosopher Jean-Paul Sartre as a "useless passion." Human imagining, writes Albert Camus, yet another existentialist philosopher, condemns us to misery, for it is absurd. To him, we long for goodness, beauty, and kindness in a world perpetually marred by evil, ugliness, and injustice.

But for the Erotic mystic of the Solomon lineage, our erotic imaginings of a world of justice and peace are the immanence of God in our lives. Our creative discontent, which drives us to imagine an alternative reality, is the image/imagination of God beating in our breast. The cosmos is pregnant with hints that guide our imaginings. We are called to heal the world in the image of our most beautiful flights of fancy. The Eros of imagination is the elixir of God running through the universe.

The Zohar is radically audacious, but potent and precise in portraying man creating God in his image—that is to say, in man's imagination. Unlike for the philosopher Ludwig Feuerbach, who called human imaginings of God mere projection, for the Zohar such imagination simply reinforces the substantive reality of God. While there is a limited truth in saying that God is a figment of human imagination, we need to remember that imagination is a figment of God.

The power of imagination is its ability to give form to the deep truths and visions of the inner divine realm. Imagination gives expression to the higher visions of reality that derive from our divine selves. Language and rational thinking are generally unable to access this higher truth. But the imagination is our prophet, bringing us the word of the Infinite, which speaks both through us and from beyond us.

imagination

the sexual models the erotic:

One of the core qualities of the sexual is fantasy. Virtually every man and woman have sexual fantasies. To fantasize means simply to imagine. Sex models Eros because in the sexual we learn the power of fantasy.

So why in modern usage does the word "fantasy" first and foremost conjure up images of the sexual? We very rarely talk about economic, political, or social fantasies. Just like the adjective "erotic," the verb "fantasize" has found itself relegated to the narrow confines of the merely sexual. The reason is clear. In modernity we have lost much of our ability to make visible—to imagine—the deeper visions of the spirit. It is mainly only in sex where we use imagination to conjure up images of that which is hidden or not revealed.

Our English word "fantasy" derives from the Greek word phantasia, which derived from a verb that meant "to make visible, to reveal." For the Greeks, fantasizing had nothing to do with sex. It meant "a making visible (through imagining) the world of the gods," the realm of pure spirit and forms.

We have the ability through imagination
to actually
reimagine the world in a very powerful way.

Imagination is an erotic quality.
It is an inner way of visioning, of imagining,
which is the source and the path to Eros.
The prophet is the one who imagines a different world. That's what prophecy is all about.
The ability to reimagine the world.

The Eros of imagination is the elixir of
God running through the universe.

crisis of imagination

The greatest crisis of our lives is neither economic, intellectual, nor even what we usually call religious. It is a crisis of imagination. We get stuck on our path because we are unable to reimagine our lives differently from what they are right now.

The most important thing in the world, implies wisdom master Nachman of Bratzlav, is to be willing to give up who you are for who you might become.

It is only in the fantasy of reimagining that we can change our reality. It is only from this inside place that we can truly change our outside. The path of true wisdom is not necessarily to quit your job, leave your home, and travel across the country. Often such a radical break indicates a failure rather than a fulfillment of imagination. True wisdom is to change your life from where you are, through the power of imagination.

The cosmos is pregnant with hints that guide our imaginings. We are called to heal the world in the image of our most beautiful flights of fancy.

Imagination is powerful. Very powerful. "Think good and it will be good," wrote Menachem Mendel Schneerson, the last master of Chabad mysticism. This is true not merely because of the psychological power of positive thinking, but also because every imagining gives birth to something real that eventually manifests itself in the universe.

For the Kabbalist, imagination is not childish. It is the spiritual reality called forth by the sacred child within.

The invitation to freedom, to personal liberation, to national liberation, is through the lens of imagination.

In our interpretation, human beings participate in divine imagination and are thus invited to be the artisans of their lives. The raw materials, colors, and dimensions of your life's canvas are a given. How you mix the colors, weave the material, even choose the picture to draw on the canvas, is your artistic privilege and obligation. To be the artist of your own life—to be your own creator—is both the highest level of the sacred and the most profound expression of our glorious, our wondrous, humanity.

imagination - detail

THE SEVENTH FACE

perception

7

By God, when you see your beauty
You will be the idol of yourself.
-Rumi

Poetry and love are intimately related because poetry, like love, is an art of perception.

The radical realization of the Erotic mystics in the lineage of Solomon teaches that love and Eros are skills that are modeled by the sexual. Sex is our teacher. Those very qualities are what teach us—in all aspects of our nonsexual lives—how to be great lovers. We rise in love when we learn the art of Eros.

To fully ground our point that love is a perception, we need to summon up the evocative English phrase "carnal knowledge." It is an idiom that is rooted in the translation of the biblical word yada, which in Hebrew means "perception" and "knowledge." Yet it is first used in the wisdom texts of Hebrew Eros to describe sexual knowing—carnal knowledge, as in "Adam knew Eve, his wife"—and only later to describe noncarnal, erotic perception.

The first biblical text says, "Adam knew Eve, his wife." Carnal erotic knowledge. Only later does the text say, "You shall know God with all your heart." Noncarnal erotic knowledge. This is because sex is the first level of seeing. It models the perception of loving. It is often the most potent realm in which we access perception. Thus, sexual seeing can guide us to a much deeper form of perception.

William Blake wrote:

LOVE to faults is always blind:
Always is to joy inclin'd,
Lawless, wing'd, and unconfin'd,
And breaks all chains from every mind.

Blake got it wrong, love is not blind. Love is perception. Love is the only power that allows us to see each other with even the remotest clarity. An artist is a master, love is in the details. Not in the sense of the petty particulars, but more as twentieth-century Erotic mystic of the Solomon

perception

lineage, Abraham Isaac Kook writes, "Love is 'the great art of the spirit.'" Art is where each magnified detail is part of a harmonized whole. An artist is a master at perceiving. The artist is the beholder whose eyes disclose beauty.

What is so special about the artist's eye? It is always open to the new, the never-before-noticed. We don't need to wait for Godot, an external God who will redeem us with a great new vision of truth and beauty. We merely need to unfurnish our eyes. Our eyes are furnished with old trauma, competition, greed, and jealousy that color our perception and prevent us from seeing the world clearly. But love removes that blindness.

The artist's eye, the lover's eye, is unfurnished, and the unfurnished eye sees true. It is not blinded with the opaque trappings of preconceptions and misconceptions. Eros calls us to have unfurnished eyes—not only in the very narrow realm of personal relationships but also in every arena of our lives.

the sexual models the erotic

The first great truth of Hebrew Tantra is that love at is core is not an emotion. It is a perception of another person- a perception that often arouses in its wake great and powerful emotion. The sexual always begins with a perception, usually external in nature. It is often an external perception of beauty or power. It might be the perceptive faculty of sight that arouses sexual attraction. But it could just as well be touch, hearing, smell, or taste. Any of these may arouse an emotional, intellectual, or even chemical attraction. As with sex, so with love and Eros.

Love is also initiated by perception, albeit an internal perception. It is the ability to see, to intuit, to sense, the infinite divine specialness, the divine point, in the beloved.

The Erotic mystics of the Solomon lineage took it one step farther. They taught that there is a deeper form of sexual arousal that is provoked not by the perception of physical beauty, but by the perception of love.

When done consciously, sexual gazing leads to a deeper lover's perception. Love is the perception of the Shechinah in the other.

"All Eros from the sexual to pure love is of the same essence," wrote the nineteenth century mystical master Nachum of Chenobyl. It is therefore possible to transpose sexual looking into the wondrous perception of love. The sexual models the erotic; this is the Secret of the Cherubs.

Receiving the Shechina is perceiving and receiving the divine point of beauty that dwells in each person. Eros and ethics become one.

revealers of the divine

Tolstoy understood that love is the perception of the soul's nakedness. To love someone is to see them in all the rawness of their authenticity, that is to say, in their divinity.

> *"What's the good of man unless there's a glimpse of a God in him? And what's the good of woman unless she's a glimpse of a Goddess of some sort?*
> *-D. H. Lawrence*

the kabbalists were often referred to as "the lookers" or "seers."

To get a handle on what that might mean, just imagine how we feel when someone looks at us with erotic, loving eyes. We feel energized, uplifted, and embraced. We become more vibrant, audacious, and alive. We feel safer in the world. The sense of alienation, separateness, and loneliness of our empty days and painful nights seems to lift. The steadier the loving gaze is, the more we can steady ourselves and chart our direction and purpose on the path of being.

It is the essence of the Holy of Holies: to become a lover and a seer. To love is to become God's verb. To love is to see with God's eyes.

THE EIGHTH FACE

giving & receiving

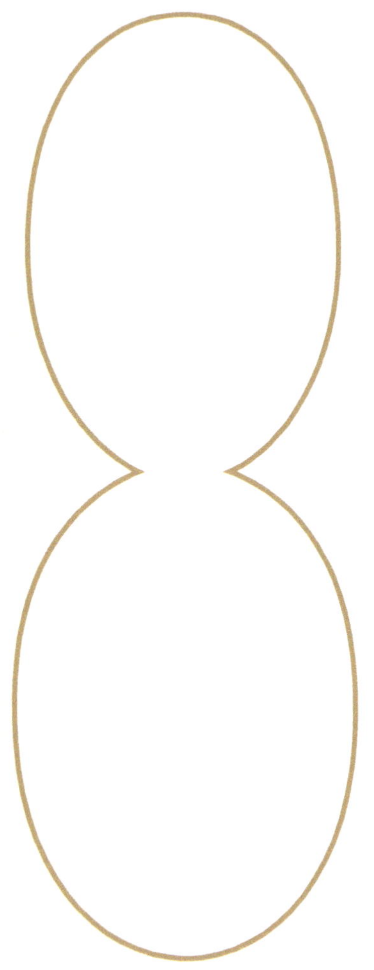

It is through the consistent commitment to the growth of the other—expressed through regular and spontaneous acts of giving—that you become a lover. Slowly over time, in a gradual expanding of self, you are able to regain and surpass even the initial ecstasy of falling in love. The ego boundaries dissolve, self is expanded to include the beloved, and the true intimacy of shared identity is achieved.

This is the spiritual dynamic of lovers. The beloved could be a man, woman, child, community, vocation, location, animal, or cause. The principle remains the same. There is no loving without giving. Love always involves the willingness to transcend self for the sake of the growth of another. This is what the romantic philosopher Goethe refers to when he says, "The sum which two married people owe to one another defies calculation. It is an infinite debt, which can only be discharged through all eternity."

For the Erotic mystics of the Solomon lineage, love is self-transcendence: the ability to break the walls of your narrow persona in order to embrace a wider understanding of self. To love another means to create a new shared identity that is larger than your individual identities. And yet the integrity of each independent "other" is maintained. Love is the great and wonderful paradox of shared identity and powerful individuality. So self-transcendence is the widening of self through consistent giving and commitment to the growth of your beloved.

For the Erotic mystics of the Solomon lineage, the word for "love" itself expresses this notion of giving, which they so cherished. "Love" in the original Hebrew is ***ahava***, derived from the word ***hav***. The primary meaning of ***hav*** is "giving." Wonderfully, in the original Hebrew, "love" and "giving" are the same word.

Every human being is born incomplete. True birth takes place over the course of a lifetime and not at life's inception. There is nothing more tragic than to die before being born. A lover is a midwife. To be a midwife is to be committed to helping your beloved birth his or her highest self. This is the great gift of love.

the evolution of intimacy

The evolution of intimacy is when the causes and people we love extend beyond our own immediate survival circle. Egocentric love is when I experience a felt sense of care and concern for myself and the people I need to survive. Ethnocentric love is when I experience a felt sense of care of concern for my entire people. My people might be my fellow citizens, my coreligionists, or any larger affiliation beyond those that I know directly. This is the evolution of intimacy from egocentric to ethno- centric. Love evolves again to world-centric when I experience a felt sense of care and concern for every human being on the planet. Finally, love evolves yet again when I experience a felt sense of care and concern not only for human beings but for all of reality. This has been called cosmo-centric love.

circles of intimacy, circles of influence

The major reason that we stop giving and loving beyond our circle of protection is that it hurts too much. We know that if we open our hearts, they will all too often get trampled and trashed.

We basically feel powerless and that we cannot really change anything. Once that belief is internalized, a self-protective mechanism kicks in. We cannot tolerate a situation in which our circle of caring is far larger than our circle of influence. When we feel that our ability to experience hurt is far greater than our ability to alleviate the pain, then we simply turn off. The dissonance becomes too great to bear. The gap between our perceived ability to be hurt and to help is simply too wide to traverse. So we narrow our circles of intimacy to only those we feel we have the ability to help. But to do so, especially in a world where graphic images of pain daily invade our lives, we need to shut down our hearts. Powerlessness corrupts. We need to know that each of us by ourselves, and even more powerfully as a community, can make a difference for love.

the mathematics of eros

If you were to enter your bank, ask a teller to withdraw fifty dollars from your account, then ask her to record it as a deposit, she would think you were joking. Then she would think you were crazy. Then she would call her manager, who would escort you out of the bank. And the bank would be right. Everyone knows depositing and withdrawing are opposite actions. To deposit is to give money into your account and to withdraw is to take money out of your account. Giving and taking are opposites, and never the twain shall meet. It's first-grade math: addition and subtraction. Everyone knows this. All the structure of economy politics and our social relations are based on this dichotomy.

Giving and receiving are opposites in nearly every sphere of our lives, yet the lover seeks to infuse this sharp and angular world with the softer curves of intimacy. The lover wants to transcend and transform the rules of first-grade math. The model for the lover? The sexual. In sex, giving and receiving follow very different rules and flow very differently.

the sexual models the erotic : giving and receiving are one

Not only is sexual love the model for radical giving, but it also personifies a very particular kind of generosity, one that defies all other giving patterns. In sex, we transcend the world of win-win, common goals, give-and-take, and

giving & receiving

getting even. The sexual models a different order of reality, where giving and receiving are indistinguishably one.

Sex is at its highest when your partner not only knows how to give you pleasure but is a master at receiving it as well. In your beloved's receiving of pleasure, you are given a great gift. In the sexual, the rigid boundaries between giving and receiving are so dramatically blurred that the two become virtually indistinguishable. Sexuality at its highest collapses the separate spheres of giving and receiving into an undulating, rhythmic flow of union. It is a great leap beyond the give-and-take of business into the virtual identity of giving and receiving within every pleasured gesture.

The sexual models a reality where the giver himself is deeply aware of how, in the very act of giving, he has received. Similarly, the receiver herself feels that in the very act of receiving, she has been privileged to give. In erotic living, withdrawals become your deposits… and giving is the greatest gift.

It was Aphra Behn, the first Englishwoman to earn her living by her writing in the mid-seventeenth century, who captured the subversive nature of erotic exchange.

I saw 'em kindle with Desire,
While with soft Sighs they blew the Fire;
Saw the Approaches of their Joy,
He growing more fierce and she less coy…
His panting Breast to hers now joined,
They feast on Raptures unconfined;
Vast and luxuriant! such as prove
The Immortality of Love.
For, who but a Divinity
Could mingle Souls to that Degree;
And melt them into Ecstasy

Behn's point is that the classical split between giving and receiving could neither "mingle souls to that degree" nor cause "his panting breast to hers now joined." It is only the sexual that models the possibility of a new vision of Eros, in which giving and receiving collapse ecstatically into one.

the secret of the kiss

The Kabbalists viewed kissing as the highest model of Eros. The teaching, called by initiates sod haneshika (meaning "secret of the kiss"), references two modes of communication. The first is speech. Although there are many levels of speech, they all suffer from one weakness: the subject-object dichotomy between giver/receiver and speaker/listener remains in place. The very act of having to speak implies a sharp separation between two souls.

The second mode of communication the teaching identifies is kissing. When the Zohar says that "nat [intimacy] is only found in the mouth," it refers not to speech but to the kiss. Kissing is the level of communication speech naturally flows into in the context of a sacred relationship. Kissing is the ideal communion.

In a wonderful rereading of a Talmudic text, one mystic interprets the rabbinic admonition of "you shall not talk too much to women" to mean "don't talk when you should already be kissing." In the kiss, the yawning gap between subject and object, giving and receiving, is bridged. The split dissolves. This is the erotic model of union. Thus the great love epic of erotic mysticism, the Song of Songs, opens with the fantasy, "Kiss me from the kisses of your mouth, for your love is more wonderful to me than wine."

In the mystical reading of this verse, what is intended is a yearning for erotic union beyond the sexual. There is a longing for the life of the kiss, where the hard and brittle boundaries of ego are softened and smoothed. This happens only in the secret of the kiss, where in every transaction both parties give and receive simultaneously.

THE NINTH FACE

surrender

Human beings are educated to be in control all the time. Many of the messages we receive, beginning with early childhood, are that we must be in control. The first conflict with our instinctive natures is, for most toddlers, toilet training. We are taught to control our bowel movements. This is but the first step in a lifetime that will constantly demand we be in control. From early on in life we are rewarded for doing this. We get painful disapproval, or worse, when we fail to exercise control. One of the most damaging assessments one can hear about a person is, "He's out of control." The mantra hammered into our psyches is: "Get ahold of yourself. Control yourself!"

While control education could be accomplished a bit more gently, we all recognize its importance. Going with the flow has its limitations. Few of us want to live in a world where people let their bowel movements (or any other impulses) flow naturally without any restraint whatsoever. Civilization is built on the lucid understanding that the world cannot survive without systematic self-control. In the life of the individual, the ability to delay gratification and channel energy and impulses is the key to a richer and deeper life. As all jelly bean devotees know, five jelly beans are delicious. On the other hand, uncontrolled consumption—three hundred jelly beans in one sitting, for example—will make you very sick.

"Who is a hero?" ask the wisdom masters. "He who controls his impulses." In the hero's journey, control and discipline are what create ethical human beings. Moreover, exercising tight control is at least one stretch in the road toward transformation. It is true that, initially, control adds some pressure to our lives. It is worth remembering, though, that coal only becomes a diamond when subjected to significant pressure. Control is and should be part of our understanding of the heroic life. But this is where the popular Western educational myth usually ends, when in truth, this is really just the beginning of the story.

the sexual models the erotic : surrender

Great sex is about giving up control. Giving up control is not about an unholy submission where you are giving up your power. To submit is to give up the power that is the dignity of your being, invested in you by reality itself. Submission, however, is very different from surrender. In surrender, you give up the artifice of your posturing and claim the power of your authentic self. The sexual models the erotic, for it is in the sexual that we learn the art of holy surrender. Giving up control in sex is holy surrender where the ego is bracketed and you are actually lived as love.

But surrender is not an abdication of power. Quite the opposite. The capacity to surrender is the greatest power that one can possess. The great paradox is that the more powerful you are, the more you refuse to submit and the deeper your surrender. Never submit other than when it is necessary as a momentary strategy; always surrender, for that is your highest sacrament.

the sexual models the erotic : sexual theater

One way in which the sexual might model the erotic is what we refer to as sexual theater—intentional role-playing in sexuality—as an approach to working with the deeper dynamics in your relationships or life. Sexual theater is also a core practice in our Tantra school.

One of the major forms of sexual theater is in the play of domination and submission in sex. We talk extensively about this form of boundary-breaking sex in our book Sexually Incorrect. For now, it is enough to say that playing intentionally with power dynamics through sexual theater can be profoundly transformative in a person's relation to power, both wielding power and surrendering to power, in every other dimension of life. The sexual models the erotic. It is in this play that we access the power of surrender in our bodies. Submission is transformed from a standard S&M practice to the holy surrender of ecstatic devotion and delight.

music and helpmates

One of the places where we overcome alienation and step inside an act of surrender is in the sacred realm of music. Song and music are erotic. We plunge into our depths even as we surrender ourselves to the sound. Eros cuts through ego and touches essence. We feel alive and totally present in the fullness of our longing.

Mastery in song and music takes place precisely at the point where radical discipline and control are transcended. At the intersection between control and surrender, the singer or musician gives herself up, allowing herself to be played by the universe. It is, of course, not an accident that an essential component of the temple service was music. The text reads, "If you are searching for Shechinah," then come to the temple with its symphony of holy song. Through music from exotic instruments and songs that opened the heart, the people were aroused to the erotics of desire and personal surrender.

It is in the music of relationship, however, that giving up control is most important. As British philosopher Adam Phillips said, "It is only when two people forget themselves in the presence of the other, that they can remember each other."

Man is lonely. In the sacred text of Solomon, God makes him a helpmate, kenegdo, "opposite him," or in some translations, "a helpmate against him." "Now what does that mean, a partner who is against him?" asks virtually all of biblical commentary. The Hebrew word used is ezer, a "helper." If she is a helpmate, then how can she also be kenegdo, "against him"? Adam is lonely. The only way beyond loneliness is love. Love is the opposite of control. If the relationship is one of domination and control, it will fail

surrender

on two levels. First, both sides will remain lonely. Second, they will not help each other, for an equal partnership is premised on giving up control. It is only if he respects her kenegdo, her opposition, her "no," that there can be love and partnership.

Whenever you insist on control in a love relationship, there are two reasons why you ruin the love. First, because only mutuality can redeem you from loneliness. Second, because love is a perception, and domination always blurs perception. This is why I often refer to our Edenic couple as "Adam and Even," for the point of Eve being a helpmate "against" is that Adam must view her as even to himself, or the relationship is doomed. When you are not kenegdo, when you are not face-to-face at the same level, you simply cannot see each other with clarity.

naming, nakedness, cleaving

Sometimes it helps to survey the results of past relationships to understand the deep necessity of giving up control. Before Eve was created, God brought Adam the animals to name. Naming, in this context, was a symbol of control. These were not intimate, affectionate names. The context was similar to the taxonomist naming animals zoologically as an act of classification and control. Rashi, the eleventh-century interpreter of the Talmud, suggests that Adam did not merely name the animals. Mythically, "naming" implies that Adam had sexual relations with all the animals. The image suggested is sexuality as conquest, sexuality without giving up control. The animals, in this reading, become symbols of sex divorced from love and Eros. Adam wanted to know if sexuality by itself was sufficient to redeem him from his loneliness.

The answer? "Man did not find among all the animals an ezer kenegdo—a partner opposite." After the sex, Adam merely felt his loneliness all the more acutely. So God caused Adam to fall asleep, a powerful myth image of vulnerability. Then in the first recorded surgery in history, God removed the rib from which Eve would be formed. The point is clear: only by giving up control and being literally opened up and exposed can an authentic relationship develop. What's more, it is only by giving up a part of your being, in this case symbolized by Adam's rib, that you can hope to overcome the infinite ache of loneliness. Only vulnerability and sacrifice can create the connection and lift you out of your loneliness.

Man and woman are described as being "naked and not ashamed." With each other they are able to be totally vulnerable, exposed, and unembarrassed. To be naked means to let go of the need for posturing. By contrast, if someone falls in love with your outer facade, you remain lonely because deep down you know the person your lover adores is not you at all.

"Man cleaved to woman, and they were one flesh," says the text. "One flesh" is an obviously sexual image. "Cleaved," which is a translation of the Hebrew devekut, is a word of the spirit connoting Eros and deep love. Once man gives up his striving for domination and control, once he is ready to create a relationship of mutuality where each side challenges the other in love to higher growth, only then is loneliness transcended into union and love. Love is a surrender, a relinquishing of control. Love of God is responding in trust to the loving force of being—the God-flow in the universe. Love of an other is responding in trust to the divinity of the other.

where lovers gaze

Love means mutuality. Neither side can have a controlling vision. We recently heard of a mother whose son very much wanted to be a writer. For years, though, for not fully understandable reasons, he was unable to get it together and write. Finally one day, on the verge of despair, he broke down crying to his mother. He told her that he was going to abandon writing. To his surprise, she said to him, "I have been waiting for you to give up writing all these years. I know it isn't right for you. Indeed, I pray every day that you should not write."

This is a story that sends shivers down our spines. Naturally the poor guy can't get a word out! And his mother, of course, does not love him at all! We are told that Saul, the first king of Israel, loved young David very much. Yet when he tells David, after the latter has slain Goliath, "You shall not return home but shall eat at the king's table," the reader knows that something is amiss. If Saul is attempting to control David, then he cannot love him. Trouble lies ahead. In due course, jealousy emerges, and Saul spends much of his later years in pathetic attempts to have David killed. As soon as the desire to control enters the story, it is only a matter of time until love fails.

In the classic lover's model, the two lovers look deeply into each other's eyes. This lasts for as long as they are still head over heels in love.

But eventually, in ordinary love, the magic fades, and then the struggles for control begin. Looking into each other's eyes changes to staring each other down. The dominant personality in the relationship usually determines the controlling vision that guides them forward.

For true erotic lovers, though, relationship is based on something more than long, melting looks while gazing into each other's eyes. Such looks are the magic and mystery of soul mate relationship and here is the great heresy of the Erotic mystics of Solomon lineage, is insufficient to sustain love. We need to move soulmates to what we will call whole mates. They come together based on erotic attraction for each other, but sustain the relationship with the Eros of shared values and vision. Lovers who don't share a higher vision, who don't work toward a common higher purpose, end up in ferocious battles for control.

the eros of surrender

It was the sensual Persian poet Hafiz who understood the full power of erotic surrender in every arena of life. The ecstatic poem "Tripping Over Joy" transmits something about the power of surrender:

What is the difference
Between your experience of Existence
And that of a saint?
The saint knows
That the spiritual path
Is a sublime chess game with God
And that the Beloved
Has just made such a fantastic move
That the saint is now continually
Tripping over Joy
And bursting out in Laughter
And saying, "I Surrender!" I couldn't regulate
spacing correctly on the poem
Whereas, my dear,
I am afraid you still think
You have a thousand serious moves.

In the sense of holy surrender, as the mark of the enlightened one that Blake referred to when he wrote in his poem Loosing and Loosening Control.

He who binds to himself a joy
does the winged life destroy;
But he who kisses the joy as it flies
Lives in eternity's sunrise.

invitation to vulnerability

What is unique about sexual love is that lovers not only let go of their internal controls but they also invite their lovers to witness their surrender. In the invitation to the other to both participate and witness, there is not only a giving up but also a giving over of some dimension of control to the beloved. To love—in all arenas of living—is not only to relinquish control but also to grant a measure of control to the other—that is to say, to be utterly openly vulnerable.

The moment we cross the line into the world of love, we have to let down some of the walls. We can be hurt. We have invited the other into our Holy of Holies in the trust and faith that she will tread gently. The uncertainty (and vulnerability) inherent in giving up control is inseparable from the invitation to love.

Deep down, the knower in us understands that love and what society labels as power are two very different, virtually opposite, modes of being. To love is to give up control and to expose our vulnerability. Power is to maintain control and hide vulnerability. In love, my gain is your gain. In power, my gain is your loss. In love, the goal is to serve and the grail is intimacy. In power, the objective is conquest and the trophy domination.

The soul longs for loss of control. There is a part of us that wants to give up the charade of constantly thinking, planning, and directing our lives. We sense intuitively that there is some deep part of us that can be revealed only when we "loosen the reins" and give up control.

Sexuality can become a sacrament modeling of our true position in the world. We no longer need to chase it compulsively to remind us that we matter. We give up the need for obsessive control. In that surrender, the world comes alive. And so it is in life, since sex models Eros. In surrender, we inherit the kingdom.

The only way beyond loneliness is love.
Love is the opposite of control.

Love of God is responding in trust to the loving force of being—the God-flow in the universe.
Love of another is responding in trust to the divinity of the other.

THE TENTH FACE

play & lishmah

The next quality of love and Eros modeled by the sexual is play. Play is close in meaning to what the Erotic mystics of Solomon lineage called lishmah, which is usually translated as "for its own sake." We are engaged in the erotic when we do something simply for its own sake—when we stop networking and let go of goal-oriented thinking, when the activity itself is the end and not the means. This is the Eros of self-evident meaning. Lishmah is when loving is the motive, for the only ulterior motive of Eros is love. Indeed, the litmus test of true love is that it has no ulterior motive. It stands and endures for its own sake. Lishmah!

the eros of play : for its own sake

To be erotically engaged means to be on the inside, totally filled and satisfied by the activity itself rather than using it as a way of getting somewhere or doing something else. The model for this kind of radical "in and of itself" engagement is the sexual. The sexual invites us inside to its fullness, promising at its highest not a networking opportunity but the richness of the experience itself. Advancement is not the issue; lishmah is not goal-oriented. Once you are in the erotic, you have arrived; you are already there. This is the endpoint. There is nowhere else to go. The process itself is the goal. It is this sense that lishmah engenders ecstasy. Past and future melt away as the present swells to infinite proportions.

The sexual models lishmah and teaches us how to be lovers, living erotically in all facets of existence. Loving either a person or an activity is an end in itself and not a means. There is no expectation other than what is. There is a deep appreciation of the inherent value, wonder, and truth of each moment. The litmus test of lishmah for an interpersonal relationship is when the person you are with becomes more important than the activity you are doing. The process becomes the result.

Beauty is lishmah. A breathtaking vista, a rainbow, a sunset—they need no excuse for existing. They just are. They are beautiful and need not serve any other purpose. A perfect expression of this lishmah quality is the female breast. The rapture that the female breast has provoked in poets, painters, and biblical writers throughout the ages is fully self-validating. It is not because of infantile memories of nourishment or because of the fascination with taboo, it is just because. God is called Shaddai, a Hebrew wordplay on the word for "breasts," shaddayim. The point is not only that God nourishes, but that the essence of the Divine also lies in its being enough; it is self-validating.

Art is lishmah. It is the end itself and requires no external justification. So while we valorize the commercial businessman who is driven by profit, we tend to frown upon an artist who shares the same quality. We expect him to carry the torch of lishmah for society. The same is true of a spiritual teacher who seems driven by commercial motivation. Yes, the teacher has a right to be compensated for his efforts. But somehow we expect him not to violate the quality of lishmah, which is so essential to endeavors of the spirit.

If we expect an activity to model lishmah, we are collectively horrified when it does not. This is precisely why society never fully accepted prostitution. On a moral plane, there are certainly more ethically serious issues to engage—slander, corporate corruption, manipulative adver- tising, to name a few. Yet we hold prostitution to a different standard not because it is a violation of any overriding moral principle. Rather, it contravenes, paradoxically, an erotic principle; sex for commercial profit violates the erotic quality of lishmah.

lishmah : for the sake of the name

The erotic quality of lishmah has a second layer of meaning, which takes us even deeper. Lishmah derives from the Hebrew letters spelling sham, meaning "there." In the first understanding of lishmah (acting for its own sake), when you give up getting there, you realize you are already there.

However, sham, pronounced "shem," has a second meaning: "name." In this layer of understanding, lishmah means "for the sake of the name." In the ultimate expression of lishmah, as we will see in a few pages, this quality of lishmah is also modeled in the sexual. But before we get there, let's take a look at what "for the sake of the name" actually means. Your name is the face of God that is you and you alone. Lishmah means living for the sake of the unique God expression that is you in the world: your name!

In the deepest sense, this second meaning of lishmah, "for the sake of the name," is but a facet of the first meaning, "for its own sake." There are two steps here. First, for the sake of the name is the most profound expression of Unique Self, the fifth face of Eros. Here is the second step. This dimension of Unique Self is not so much focused on your unique gift or mission; rather, it is focused on living your name in the world. You live for the sake of your name, because that is who you are. This sense of "being yourself" or living for your name is the quality of doing things "just because." That is what it means to act for its own sake. I act just because, for the sake of my name.

This is not merely a psychological idea but a life-transforming mystical realization. "For the sake of the name" refers to your own name and to the name of God. In this realization of lishmah, you understand clearly that both names, your name and the name of God, are one. It is this sense that one lives for the sake of the name. One's actions are self-justifying and not merely instrumental.

the sexual models the erotic : for the sake of the name

The Three Texts of Orgasm

This second meaning is one in which we will see very clearly that the second quality of lishmah—for the sake of the name—is modeled most powerfully in the sexual. The importance of the name becomes obvious in sex. What do we call out at the moment of sexual climax? Three common possibilities: the first is that we cry out "Oh, God," or its equivalent in whatever the lingua franca happens to be: Elohim, mon Dieu, etc. The second possibility is that we call out the name of the beloved. The third is that we call out, "Yes." At this moment of ultimate vulnerability—and thus authenticity—there is a blurring of names. The name of the other and the name of God become almost interchangeable. Here again the sexual models the erotic, this time in the most dramatic of ways, bringing us to the heart of the cherubs' secret.

Why do God's name and the name of the beloved seem to interchange at the moment when all the outer layers are stripped bare and we call out our highest truth? Because in the deepest place, it is the same name! The name of God is no less than the name of every being from the beginning to the end of time. The "Yes" is the same "Holy Yes," which reality cries out at the moment of the original big bang that birthed reality. The "Yes" is the radical affirmation of the unrelenting goodness of life and our place in the universe. The name of God and the name of the beloved are one. Yes!

play & lishmah

in the holy of holies

Now let's go one step deeper. The sexual models the erotic. The lover crying out "Oh, God" at the height of sexual rapture models the rapture of the high priest who calls out "Oh, God" in the erotic climax of merging with the Divine, in the Holy of Holies of the Jerusalem Temple. In the Solomon lineage, the priest is the incarnation of the flow of love in the universe. The high priest in the Jerusalem Temple would enter the cherub-crowned Holy of Holies once a year. What would he do there? What was the nature of the mystery rite he performed? This was the only rite that was witnessed by the sexually entwined cherubs. So undoubtedly the mystery rite in the Holy of Holies lies at the very heart of the mystery of love.

As we already know, this day of entering the Holy of Holies is called the Day of Atonement, At-one-ment. It was a time of radical ecstasy, union, and joy. The priest is described in the Zohar as the incarnation of the male organ, while the Holy of Holies is the feminine Divine, the Shechinah. In some Zohar passages, Shechinah is the archetypal expression of the yoni.

So the mystery rite is the priest and the Shechinah merging in erotic union. What did the priest actually do in the Holy of Holies? Tradition answers unequivocally: he called out the name. Not just any name, mind you; but the unpronounceable name of God, the name that was so true and had so much power that it was never said except at this one time of great intimacy. In the ecstasy of the erotic spirit, the priest, the lover par excellence, cried out the name! Mystical orgasm, pure and simple.

In the language of Kabbalah, mystical orgasm brings the priest into the ***ayin***—"nothingness," no-thing-ness. ***Ayin*** is the bliss of leaving self behind in the rapture of orgasm. Yet when love is deep, orgasm gives way not to an empty hangover but to a sweet aftertaste. In that aftertaste the self is reborn. In calling out "Oh, God," the lover also rebirths her own name. In the little death of orgasm, self is reborn. The name of God and the name of the person are one.

In a precisely parallel image, God's face is the totality of all human faces from the beginning to the end of time. The Zohar teaches that when all the root souls who form God's will have been born, it will be the dawn of a new age of consciousness. We will have entered the Holy of Holies—otherwise known as the inside of the inside—or in an alternative reading of the same Hebrew phrase, "the face of faces."

When all human beings who form God's face have been born, we will be ***lifnei Hashem***—"before God." The deeper translation, however, is on "the inside of God's face"—or the most fully literal translation: on "the inside of the face of the name."

Your name is the face of God that is you and you alone. Lishmah means living for the sake of the unique God expression that is you in the world: your name!

Greeting someone using God's name meant acknowledging the infinite divine specialness in the other.

THE ELEVENTH FACE 11

creativity

The eleventh face of Eros is creativity—an infinite world of depth and delight entwined with agony and ecstasy. Sex is creative. Sex models Eros. The nature of Eros is ceaselessly creative. Creativity is a primary source of aliveness. The aliveness of the universe expresses itself in what Stuart Kauffman calls the inherent, "ceaseless creativity of cosmos." The cosmos moves toward ever-greater levels of emergence; it is perpetually creating. We call something a new emergent when it emerges from all that came before, even as it is greater than the sum of its parts.

Creativity wells up from another face of Eros: uniqueness. Creativity takes place when new and unique configurations of intimacy emerge on both the atomic and cellular levels. New configurations of unique intimacy between atoms and between cells is what causes every breakthrough to new levels of complexity, consciousness, and love. The new interactions are drawn forth from the cosmos by its own inherent creative intelligence, what evolutionary science refers to as the "self-organizing universe." Creativity awakens on the human level when the human being realizes his or her Unique Self. When people find their unique voice, then they become ceaselessly creative. We are not separate from the cosmos. Our creativity—an expression of our uniqueness—is simply the erotic cosmos awakening as us.

the sexual models the erotic: creativity

The radical embrace of human creativity is rooted in the Secret of the Cherubs. It is not insignificant that according to Erotic mystics of the Solomon lineage, the world was created from the empty space between the two sexually entwined temple cherubs that were perched at the top of

creativity

the covenant in Solomon's temple. This "space between" is the axis mundi, the source of all creativity. The temple, you remember, is called in the original Hebrew the mikdash, "the place of holiness." Eros is creativity is holiness.

Even more dramatically, the wisdom masters symbolically identify the Holy of Holies with the marital bed of King Solomon. The masters explain: "Just as Solomon's bed was fruitful and multiplied, so the Holy of Holies was fruitful and multiplied." Said differently, "Just as the bed of Solomon was sexually creative, so too is the Holy of Holies erotically creative." That is precisely the cherub tradition saying in its own internal parlance: the sexual models the erotic. And the erotic and the holy are one. Solomon and his archetypal temple, « a thousand wives" embody cosmic creativity performed in the flesh. Sex is the ultimate paradigm of erotic creativity. Solomon's bed was very much an epicenter of creativity. The natural creativity of the sexual is of course made self-evident in the conception and birthing of a baby. But Solomon and the cherub mystics point to the raw creativity inherent in the sexual itself. We turn to E. E. Cummings again for a taste of the intrinsic creativity of the sexual, well beyond the classical procreation of a baby.

(lady i will
touch you with my mind.)
Touch you,that is all,
lightly and you utterly will become
with infinite ease
the poem which i do not write.

Cummings evokes not just the raw physicality, but the creative gesture inherent in the erotic touch. That is what he means by "i will touch you with my mind." In the lightness of the creative erotic touch, the beloved literally becomes a new creation. In concluding the poem, Cummings describes how the beloved becomes the poem. Lovemaking is the writing of a creative poem with one's lover being the new verse.

In the last verse Cummings declares in understatement that his lover, through their sexing, has become the poem. The creative act of poetry takes place in the sexing itself as his beloved becomes the verse.

Solomon, fired by divine imagination, was the human architect of the Holy of Holies, the builder of the great edifice of Eros. Solomon understood that there was an essential connection between the sexuality of his own bed and the Eros of God's temple. This connection is precisely the Secret of the Cherubs. Sex models Eros; our bedrooms model the temples of our lives.

In its archetypal mode, sex is the ultimate paradigm of erotic creativity. What could be more erotically powerful than the creation of a new life? Indeed, creativity is so bound up with sex that many religions, classical Christianity chief among them, sanctioned sexuality only if it led to procreation. The breaking of the connection between procreation and sex was seen as a fundamental violation of the sexual ethos.

Erotic mysticism of the Solomon lineage shared the deep correlation between procreation and sex. Sex that created a child was considered ultimately sacred. However, the Solomon lineaege mystics insisted that every sexual act is creative, whether it creates a child or not. The essential nature of the sexual is creativity.

Sex always creates a new reality. Sometimes that reality expresses itself in the visible material world in the form of a child. But even when there is no physical manifestation, there is always a spiritual creation. Every sexual engagement, no matter how seemingly meaningless, births a new spiritual reality. In the old spiritual language, these new realities were thought to be either angels or demons. A deep reading of these sources shows that angels or demons are really manifestations of our inner soul processes. In this sense, there is no such thing as casual sex. Sex always has meaning and creative impact in the world of the spirit. Thus, sex models the Eros of creativity.

creativity / detail

creating god

In the Secret of the Cherubs tradition, there is no sharp demarcation between human and divine creativity. God and human live on the same continuum. That by itself is a radical affirmation of human adequacy and dignity. This is the erotic humanism that emerges from the temple tradition. But it is more than that. As we will see, human beings—rooted in their unique voice—are so creatively potent that they can even create new divinity.

In its archetypal mode, sex is the ultimate paradigm of erotic creativity. What could be more erotically powerful than the creation of a new life? Indeed, creativity is so bound up with sex that many religions, classical Christianity chief among them, sanctioned sexuality only if it led to procreation. The breaking of the connection between procreation and sex was seen as a fundamental violation of the sexual ethos.

Many of the great philosophers and mystics have gone so far as to view creativity and Eros as being identical. For Plato in The Symposium, Eros is the creative arousal that drives the world forward. Plato implicitly understands that Eros is most powerfully symbolized in sex.

sex and creativity

How does sex model erotic creativity? What is it about sex that is so essential for our inner creativity?

The answer lies in the nature of the sexual. Sexuality models Eros because sex takes us to the inside. There is a moment in sex where we let go of our observer status and fully merge with the sexual. In this moment, we access our most primal self, the self that underlies our public postures, social masks, and even rational thought. This inner self is the erotic source code of reality.

To access the inner operating system of the cosmos and be creative, the sense of separate self must be temporarily bracketed. We must re-immerse ourselves in what the mystics called "the river of light that comes from Eden." This river is the flow of Eros, the throbbing, pulsating primal energy that sustains the universe.

Our stories—each and every one of them—are part of God's story.

On the canvas of our internal spiritual, emotional, and psychological processes, as well as through our physical actions, we create God.

"Every person has their own unique letter in the sacred scroll."

dark eros

The sexual is the focal point where we touch Eros. For not only does sexuality tie us into unmediated Eros, but it also connects us to the darkness. It is through our sexuality that we meet much of our shadow.

As always, sexuality models the erotic, but it does not exhaust the erotic. The goal is to plug into these matrixes of Eros and engage in the artistic re-creation of every dimension of our lives.

This is the secret of the sexually entwined cherubs that stood at the epicenter of Eros in the Holy of Holies in the temple.

To be a great artist of self, one must access the full erotic energy of the universe. Only this energy allows you to defy inertia and create the infinitely unique being that is you.

We must re-immerse ourselves in what the mystics called "the river of light that comes from Eden." This river is the flow of Eros, the throbbing, pulsating primal energy that sustains the universe.

THE TWELFTH FACE

pleasure and delight

The twelfth face of Eros is delight, or pleasure. Eros is a pleasurable experience. Delight is a primary source of aliveness.

the sexual models the erotic:

Pleasure is another way that sexuality models Eros. Sex is the locus of pleasure. Sex and pleasure and delight are virtual synonyms in the consciousness of humanity. It is in sex that we experience the full meaning of delight. The classic poet Swinburne speaks for all of humanity when he writes:

I wist not what, saving one word—Delight.
And all her face was honey to my mouth,
And all her body pasture to mine eyes;
The long lithe arms and hotter hands than fire,
The quivering flanks, hair smelling of the south,
The bright light feet, the splendid supple thighs
And glittering eyelids of my soul's desire.

Sexual pleasure models erotic pleasure, but it does not exhaust erotic pleasure. We need to experience erotic delight in every dimension of our nonsexual lives. Further, within sex there are authentic and pseudo pleasures. The same is true for pleasure in every facet of life. Finally, the desire for sexual pleasure tells us in the most direct of terms that the cosmos evolves through delight. Reality evolves because it is pleasurable is a fair summation of the leading edges of both mysticism and contemporary science.

Moreover, pleasure is both the path and the destination. The methodology of evolution is pleasure, even as the inherent telos of evolution is the most refined pleasure for the most people. There are several distinct ideas in this sentence. First, evolution evolves because it feels good. Second, the trajectory of evolution is toward higher and deeper pleasure. The more evolved a person, the greater her capacity for pleasure. Third, the arrow of evolution is not just toward deeper pleasure but also toward more pleasure for more and more people. For example, an average person can get at Whole Foods an array of pleasure-inducing foods that were not available two hundred years ago to the king of France. Fourth, evolution's arrow aims toward more and more pleasure not only for people but also for wider and wider swaths of reality, including mammals, animals, forests, and oceans. Humane treatment of animals and saving the rain forests are but two examples. Reality moves toward more pleasure for all of existence at all levels, all the way up and all the way down the magnificent chain of being.

the eros of pleasure and delight

How to get to the pleasure modeled by sex differs for everyone, but for everyone the goal is the same. Pleasure is always the goal, even if for some of us, or for some part of us, the path to pleasure is through pain. Sex models the metaphysical truth that all creative Eros is deeply delightful. Noam elyon, "the higher sweetness," and oneg, "pleasure," are but two of a stream of Zoharic idioms that describe delight as the natural bedfellow of Eros.

The Sefer Yetzirah, the earliest known Hebrew mystical work, sets up oneg as the highest level of good. In one wisdom passage, the great question posed by God to every soul after death is: "Did you derive pleasure from my world?" This is the measure of a life well lived. To live erotically is to live in delight.

comfort versus pleasure

Pleasure, of course, is not the same as comfort. Pain is usually thought to be the opposite of pleasure. But probing more deeply, we realize this is not quite true. The opposite of pain is comfort. The goal of comfort is to avoid all pain. Pleasure always incorporates a dimension of pain. Indeed, the more profound the pleasure, the more there is potential for necessary pain. Just ask a parent to name his greatest pleasure and his greatest pain and the point becomes abundantly clear. The answer to both is invariably "my children." The essence of wisdom is the ability to distinguish between necessary and unnecessary pain. In classical sources, the goal of the future world is to "receive pleasure from the Shechinah." This future world, however, is fully available in the present.

Another example: a composer works deep into the night on a symphony only he can hear. He is ecstatic, lifted up, as he creates and refines the music revealed in his heart. His back is aching from sitting for too many hours, his eyes are heavy with exhaustion, and he's thirsty but unwilling to break his concentration to go get a drink of water. On a physical level, he experiences pain, but on the level of his emotions and spirit, he is absorbed in delight. His pleasure knows no bounds. Is he comfortable? No. Is he happy? Beyond what words can describe. The opposite of pain is comfort, not pleasure, because pleasure can coexist with pain.

The very process of evolution could be fairly described as the evolution of pleasure. The more evolved or advanced a being, the greater her capacity to experience delight. Pleasure is a skill that increases with every deepening stage of evolution.

addicts and sages

What is the difference between an addict and an enlightened sage? The enlightened sage derives virtually infinite pleasure from ordinary life. The air, colors, sounds, and fragrances of life explode upon him with delight. Similarly, human relationship for the enlightened is filled with poignancy and passion, which birth virtually infinite pleasure.

The addict, on the other hand, is unable to get pleasure from ordinary life. Indeed, the inability to derive pleasure from ordinary life is the very definition of addiction. For the addict, the pain of ordinary life is so intense that it must be covered over at all costs. Often addicts are the most sensitive among us, and for that reason they cannot bear the pain. The addict then turns to pseudo Eros—addiction in all its forms—to paper over the dearth of Eros that makes life intolerable. Thus, the healing of addiction cannot come from the classical models of recovery treatment only. Ultimately, addiction can only be healed by a return to Eros. Because addiction is pleasure unwoven, the healing of addiction can only come from pleasure rewoven. The sustained healing of addiction is directly dependent on the addict's ability to re-access delight and to re-eroticize her life.

the motivating force of existence

In the Secret of the Cherubs, pleasure is not only our birthright. It is also the motivating force of all existence. Pleasure drives the entire trajectory of emergence. In evolutionary terms, we might say that reality evolves because it feels good to do so. Not only are higher levels of evolutionary development able to have deeper experiences of pleasure, it is also true that the attractor—the motive force of the entire evolutionary process—is pleasure. This was the secret of the Holy of Holies that science is now catching up to, at least on the external level of perception. Leading-edge scientists are talking about a "quantum hedonism" as the structural nature of the cosmos. Quantum hedonism expresses at the subatomic level and appears as self-evident in our lives. We are moved by pleasure. Wisdom, however, is to truly know your pleasure, to discern between the different levels of pleasure. In a forthcoming work, I (Marc) identity seven levels of pleasure. Within each level, the goal is to cultivate discernment between authentic pleasure and pseudo pleasure. The first six levels include physical pleasure; love, affection, and relationships; standing for a cause and productive work; transformation; true knowledge; and Unique Self-creativity. At the seventh and final level, there is evolutionary pleasure—the delight of awakening as the evolutionary impulse and literally becoming, through your life and transformation, the leading edge of evolution. At this level you experience the pleasure of directly participating in the evolution of culture and consciousness.

Wisdom comes from being able to discern between genuine pleasure and pseudo pleasure. For example, at level one there is the authentic pleasure of eating delicious, healthy food versus the counterfeit pleasure of eating junk food. In the pleasure of relationships, there can be authentic intimacy or counterfeit intimacy, which may be codependent or even abusive. There's the pleasure of standing up for a good cause and the pseudo pleasure of standing for a false cause. Pseudo pleasure is but another form of pseudo Eros.

pleasure & delight

Pleasure is not opposed to ethics—precisely the opposite. When you live the erotic life, you realize that pleasure is the source of all ethics. The old Greek split between hedone ("pleasure") and daemon ("meaning") was wrong. The source of all meaning and ethics is pleasure. We need to refine our delights, however. Junk food is a fast and easy delight. If you have ever eaten truly superlative food that makes you almost faint in orgiastic ecstasy, then you know it is a different experience from grabbing a candy bar at the convenience store. Enjoying the superlative meal is not only a greater pleasure, but it also requires a far more refined capacity to experience pleasure. It is something like the difference between the pleasure a tenth-grade, average math student gets from solving a math problem and the undulating, ecstatic delight a world-class, genius mathematician like Ramanujan receives from his erotic vision of the mathematical cosmos.

The great question posed by God to every soul after death is: "Did you derive pleasure from my world?" This is the measure of a life well-lived. To live erotically is to live in delight.

- Sefer Yetzira,
in the earliest known Hebrew mystical work

On The Pain Of Eros

The sexual models the erotic is true for both the pleasure of Eros and its pain. We have talked much about how sex models Eros in all of her faces, including pleasure. Now we turn to the pain of Eros. Here, too, the sexual models the erotic. Sexuality leaves so many mortally wounded in her wake. There is so much pain from what is supposed to be the source of so much pleasure. We are confused about sexuality.

first thoughts on the pain of eros

Love is grabbing hold of the Great Lion's mane
and wrestling and rolling deep into Existence
While the Beloved gets rough
And begins to maul you alive.

There was a time when we all believed that there was a way out of the pain of Eros. Some people may believe that we didn't try hard enough; others are correct in asserting that we didn't succeed. But we can tell you that we believed, in theory, in a version of love that is fulfilled through commitment, loving gestures, and good listening skills. We thought that the dilemmas that love presents to us were solvable if we were earnest enough, practiced enough, and learned how to honestly communicate the truth of who we are and what we could offer. Unfortunately, there was a quiet untruth in this approach—not only because all of us have lied to others, but also because most of us have lied to ourselves, saying that if we got it right, we would not have to feel pain in loving.

Our approach didn't take into account the ruthless side of Eros—the aspect of Eros that does not let us cut this kind of a deal in any way, which is wildly uncompromising and insists that we live a fully embodied life, one that includes pain, loss, confusion, and bewilderment. Eros is fierce and unrelenting; it won't be captured, cajoled, or lulled into the realm of the comfortable, particularly when it is the ego trying to settle into an untrue version of love. As the Hafiz puts it:

True Love, my dear,
Is putting an ironclad grip upon
The soft, swollen balls
Of a Divine Rogue Elephant
And Not having the good fortune to Die!

The sexual models the erotic—this is true in all kinds of positive and pleasurable ways, but it is also true in terms of suffering and pain. The sexual life is filled with an array of agonies that are not easily borne by the ego, by the body, or by the identity of a small or limited self. There is the pain of not being seen or desired, and the pain of being seen starkly, in clear light of our most obvious flaws and imperfections. There is the pain of not having the attention we seek, or the pain of having it for a time, and then losing it. There is the startling pain of realizing that we are not special in the way we thought we were. Or worse, recognizing that when we thought our love was exclusive, that we are not the only one. There is the pain of others wanting more from us than we are able to give, and the pain of trying to give and not being wanted. There is the pain of love that turns to hate, of affection that turns to contempt, and of physical exchange, once desired, that becomes repellent. Then there is the overlarge, unbearable pain of betrayal. Betrayal is uniquely excruciating because only someone whom you really love—"someone who would never betray you"—can deliver this particular sad and often vicious blow.

We sometimes are called to enter so deeply into the interiority of the pain of sexual and erotic betrayal that we can no longer believe anything about anything. At these moments, sometimes moments that last in aching reality for months and even years, it hurts so much that we cannot find any ideas around it. The only thing we are able to do is to let ourselves into the feeling, to live on the inside of the pain until it clears.

Sex models life in that it hurts like hell. Eros is radical aliveness moving toward contact. Radical aliveness has a side that is excruciatingly painful. So does contact. Is it any wonder that a vigorous world of sex and pain are coupled in the common practice of S&M, and domination and submission are the two poles around which this practice revolves? We are bound—bound to inflict injury, and bound to receive it. We're sure to be hurt in love, and we're sure to hurt. We are subjected to injury against our will, and no matter how hard we fight against it, we injure others all the time. We say this not to release ourselves or others of responsibility; ignorance, hubris, and grasping demand reckoning in love, and all transgressions against others must be recognized for what they are. But genuine sensitivity, radical responsibility taking, even the vow to end suffering, do not take away pain.

The beautiful rock mystic Bono and the transcendent Mary J. Blige sing from the pain of the Irish and the black American experience:

Did I ask too much, more than a lot
You gave me nothing, now it's all I got.
We're one, but we're not the same,
Well, we hurt each other, then we do it again…

We have to be willing to look into pain first, deeply, directly. We need to know it firsthand, entering the interior of pain like we enter the interior of sex—with full presence, with a yearning to see, feel, and know it, and with a mind and heart expanded enough to embrace the whole impossibility at once. For as we saw, presence, wholeness, interiority, and yearning are the primary faces of the erotic modeled in the sexual, both in her pleasure and in her hurt.

Only a lover longs to look directly into the eyes of reality and see things exactly as they are. When we talk about spiritual courage—this is the moment. When we talk about being a lover—this is what we mean. We embrace everything exactly as it is—in excruciating, gorgeous detail. We notice how we hide, slink away, or build up a solid story of breach and betrayal. And our spiritual training again instructs us to surrender instead, to let go, to relinquish our ideas, and to breathe into the unwanted sensations. It promises to help us transcend devastating erotic experience, but in love, the only way out is through. We cannot transcend painful experiences without going through them, without becoming them.

In that realization we begin to feel the embrace of the Shechinah of Eros. She is the most expansive, compassionate, and full universal lover, holding every aspect of us at the deepest core of our being, rocking us, listening to our sobs, even as she caresses our head. The Shechinah holds us all in our pain, and in it, we meet her there. In the comfort of her arms, with the soothing sounds of her voice, pain is none other than compassion herself. "In all of their pain, I am in pain..." cries out the erotic mystic Isaiah. "Your left hand is under my head and your right hand embraces me," is ecstatically exclaimed by Solomon, who experiences more than most, the pain of the erotic and the sexual.

There is a deep core in our experience that knows how to hold others in their pain. But we do not do it nearly often enough. That deep knowing that is our birthright is what the Zohar of the Erotic mystics of the Solomon lineage call the "Shechinah that is I." That knowing is God. It is the same as going into the pleasure so extremely, surrendering and opening to it so you become it. And in that merging with the full openness to love and pain—because it is you—you feel the luminous nothingness of all that is.

We, all of us, must be willing now to feel hurt, and the deepest hurt is the recognition of having hurt others. Rumi said it

The sadness I have caused any face
by letting a stray word
strike it, any pain
I have caused you,
what can I do to make us even—
Demand a hundred fold of me—I'll pay it.

Whenever you truly collapse into the pain, when you surrender into the hurt, whether yours or of others, what always happens is that you feel the embrace of the feminine. The pain, if you're truly to enter its inside, always gives way to the Shechinah's embrace. If you are willing to feel so deeply into the pain that you no longer exist, then you meet God in pain. No being should ever die without feel like he is being held by the lover, by the feminine, by the Shechinah.

This is called by the erotic mystics of the Kabbalah, to participate with pain of the Shechinah in exile. We we meet the Shechinah in our pain. "In all of their pain I am in pain," cries out the Erotic mysticof the Solomon lineage, Isaiah. This is the "Shechinah that is called I." When you recognize that she is you and you carry that quality into the world, you bring redemption to yourself, the world, and the Shechinah. You bring the redemption that always was and already is. To enter the pain in this way, you must, at least for a time, give up the protest. Give up your ideas about what and how people should act and what people should do. That is the teaching of forgiveness. That is the teaching of love.

taken by love

It is Bono who knows to sing of the pain of Eros:

one love, one life, when it's one need in the night.

Whenever there is need there is pain. Because there is no one person who can ever fill our emptiness, the pain of unmet needs always accompanies the erotic encounter with other.

Did I disappoint you
or leave a bad taste in your mouth?

The illusion that separate selves can meet and find ultimate oneness is shattered in the realization of separation. Knowing that we are "not the same" must always come before the tenderness of true love that has the capacity to stay open through the pain.

We're one, but we're not the same.
We get to carry each other,
carry each other

Bono, in verse after verse, evokes the impossibility of loving, which must always be recognized before love's true possibility is born.

Have you come here for forgiveness,
Have you come to raise the dead,
Have you come here to play Jesus
to the lepers in your head

He returns again and again to the poignant realization of separation which must always precede true bliss.

We're one, but we're not the same.
Well, we hurt each other, then we do it again.

It is more then mere pain, however. We often feel degraded and humiliated in love. Being willing to bear the ego's humiliation is a pre- requisite for great love.

You ask me to enter,
but then you make me crawl

To receive another in love is to be willing to bear the ecstasy of their pain.

And I can't keep holding on to what you got,
when all you got is hurt.

Once you realize that there is no escaping the pain of Eros, you can then settle in to the fierce grace of commitment.

One life, but we're not the same.
We get to carry each other,
carry each other.

All phenomena arise from this one source, and the body is none other than God. All of our spiritual traditions, in however many different forms, show us that everything is one thing... one beautiful, radical, unknowable and ungraspable, vast, empty gorgeousness... and that nothing, absolutely nothing, needs to be rejected. This is the enlightenment born of pain. In the universality of pain is the democratization of enlightenment. It is an enlightenment we all must share, for its knowing can end the pain.

If we learn to live wide open, even as we are hurt by love, then the Divine wakes up to its own true nature of love. To be firm in your knowing of love even when you are desperate, to be strong in your knowing of forgiveness even when you betray and are betrayed, this is what it means to be holy. Sufi mystic Rabia said it beautifully in "It Acts Like Love":

My body is covered with wounds this world made,
but I still long to kiss Him, even when God said,
"Could you also kiss the hand that caused each
scar, for you will not find me until you do."

Murder of Eros

It is the collapse of Eros that leads to what we have called the murder of Eros. Wilhelm Reich called this "the murder of Christ". By "Christ" he meant Eros or life force. This is one of the most common but hidden dimensions of human existence. To live an erotic life, we must guard against the murder of Eros. This is a fundamentally denied yet ever-present human impulse. Human beings may be ready to confess many sins, but all feign innocence when accused of the murder of Eros. And yet this primal impulse is as old as civilization itself. What has changed, however, is that because the murder of Eros is no longer socially acceptable, the impulse is carefully disguised.

It is what moves Cain to murder Abel. It is what has always moved ambitious but broken princes to kill their father the king. The human feeling that moves a person to murder Eros is called malice. The murder of Eros is motivated by some combination of greed, envy, and rage. These are the three ingredients that nourish malice.

Malice is always filled with projection onto, and distortion of, the object of malice. Authentic victims must always be protected.

Malice is both the polar opposite of Eros as well as one of the most sophisticated forms of pseudo- Eros.

Wilhelm Reich calls the murder of Eros "the emotional plague of man". When the emotional plague strikes its victim, it strikes hard and fast. It strikes without mercy or regard for truth or facts or anything else except one thing: to kill the victim.

When the plague kills, it kills for wretched reasons. Therefore, to assure the murder, it will not permit weighing accusation against the true, full being of the victim. It will tear down the victim's honor, besmirch every bit of innocent intention or act; it will pronounce innocuous details in a tone and with a slant of intonation which is meant to kill the last vestige of love or esteem for the victim in the hearts of the most devoted friends.

In literature we think of historical archetypes like Iago and Othello. In music we think of the movie Amadeus and its archetypical depiction of Salieri and Mozart. In both cases, the Eros of the object of malice causes a collapse in the Eros of the perpetrator of malice.

None of this is surprising. Malice elicits forceful attacks and even what psychologists in the field have called "annihilating behavior". Malice is not connected with legitimate causes at is core—it always hides behind them. It is fed by what the leading British psychoanalyst Joseph Berke calls a distorted "inner world of fact and fantasy, brought about by confused interplay of perception, memory and imagination".

the perpetrator of malice is recognizable by seven identifying characteristics

1: its obsessive and virtually undying nature

2: the wild exaggeration and distortion of the person against whom the malice is aimed, coupled with an utter denial of any and all goodness that he or she might possess

3: action is taken, often deadly action, without talking to both sides of the conflict and without checking basic facts or underlying motivations.

4: radical demonization of the object of malice.

5: the ascription of virtually occult-like powers to the object of malice, coupled with the infantilizing of his or her ostensible victims.

6: active process of manufacturing victims, all of whom receive significant social and psychological reward.

7: fostering a group-think context in which "the victims" or "the women" or "the community" speak as a collective in order to avoid personal responsibility.

The core identifying characteristic of the people of malice is that they attack, undermine, or demonize others instead of facing their own internal virulence.

"It is certain that envy is the worst sin that is: for all others sin against one virtue, whereas envy is against all virtue and all goodness."

-Geoffrey Chaucer

It is absolutely necessary to liberate the world from malice in order to allow Eros and love to flourish.

Envy is often a vicious streak in an otherwise decent and even good personality.

Malice is a primal form of rivalry that hides an obsessively dark and carefully hidden pseudo- Eros.

murder of eros

About The Authors

dr. marc gafni

Gafni is a visionary thinker, social activist, and passionate philosopher. He is known for his "source code teachings," including Unique Self theory and the Five Selves, the Amorous Cosmos, A Politics of Evolutionary Love, A Return to Eros and Digital Intimacy. He is author of twenty-five books, of which the first ten have been published, including the award-winning Your Unique Self: The Radical Path to Personal Enlightenment. He holds a doctorate in philosophy from Oxford University, as well as Orthodox rabbinic ordination.

One cultural critic described Gafni as "a cross between Einstein, Da Vinci and Rumi, with a dash of Robin Williams" working at the cutting edge of the New Narrative, collaborating with a team of thinkers articulating a new vision of meaning for the world. "Gafni thinks in highly complex terms but speaks simply and directly."

Gafni is playing a pivotal role in evolving a new 'dharma,' or meta-theory of meaning overflowing with heart – a new set of distinctions, that is helping to re-shape key pivoting points in global consciousness and culture.

He teaches on the cutting edge of philosophy and spirit in the West, with the aim of participating in the articulation of what Dr. Gafni together with Dr. Zak Stein and colleagues are calling CosmoErotic Humanism.

At the core of CosmoErotic Humanism is what Dr. Gafni and Dr. Stein are calling 'First Principles and First Values,' Anthro-Ontology and a "Universal Grammar of Value."

This is the ground of a new shared universe story and a new narrative of identity for the new human and the new humanity. This is what they are calling the emergence from Homo sapiens to Homo Amor.

This shared story rooted in First Principles and First Values can then serve as the matrix for a global ethos for a global civilization.

Dr. Gafni is the Co-Founder, together with Ken Wilber and Sally Kempton, of the Center for Integral Wisdom where he serves as its co-President. Together with Dr. Zak Stein, they are co-leading a team of thinkers, articulating a new vision of meaning for the world. The Center is a leading activist think tank dedicated to articulating a practical politics of evolutionary love, and to catalyzing an emergent personal and global vision of ethics, Eros and meaning. Former Board Chairs include the pre-eminent futurist Barbara Marx Hubbard, John P. Mackey of Whole Foods, Kate Maloney, Lori Galperin, Carrie Kish and other esteemed thought and business leaders. Our current chairs are Shareef Malnik and Gabrielle Anwar.

Dr. Gafni is the Evolutionary Scholar in Residence – and since Barbara's Marx Hubbard's passing, the Director – at the Foundation for Conscious Evolution and a co-founder of the Integral Evolutionary Tantra Institute and the Outrageous Love Project with Dr. Kristina Kincaid. He is co-founder of the Unique Self Institute with Claire Molinard. All of these entities function under the larger umbrella of the Office for the Future, co-founded by Barbara Marx Hubbard, Marc Gafni, Zachary Stein, and co-chaired by Stephanie Valcke and Ivan Bossuyt. Marc Gafni currently serves as the President of the Office for the Future.

Over the past 30 years, Dr. Gafni has developed evolutionary and activist programs rooted in his commitment to what he has termed "participating in the evolution of love." Together with author and social innovator Barbara Marx Hubbard, he has been working on a series of new works revolving around Evolutionary Spirituality.

Together with the late Barbara Marx Hubbard he co-founded One Mountain, Many Paths. The group gathers weekly every Sunday as A Global Communion of Pioneering Souls committed to articulating First Principles and First Values: A New Story for a New Humanity. Or as Marc and Barbara said together, A Planetary Awakening in Love through Unique Self Symphonies.

A Rabbinic lineage holder in Bible, Talmud, and Kabbalah, Gafni self-describes as a "citizen" of both the new lineage of World Spirituality even as he has remained loyal to the classical Hebrew lineage practices in which he was raised. He has been an editor of the Journal of Integral Theory and Practice on issues of Integral spirituality and a faculty member of J.F.K. University.

Gafni has initiated multiple leading-edge visionary programs including writing and hosting the leading National Television show on Ethics and Spirit in the Middle East, and initiated the Success 3.0 Summit and movie with John Mackey and Kate Maloney whose method and movement was to bring together key thought leaders and change agents to collaboratively evolve a bold new Integral vision of success, rooted in the entrepreneurial values of Wake Up, Grow Up, Show Up, and Evolutionary Love.

Learn more about Dr. Gafni's teaching at:

www.officeforthefuture.com
www.centerforintegralwisdom.org
www.marcgafni.com
www.WhoIsMarcGafni.com

dr. kristina kincaid

Dr. Kristina Kincaid is a Speaker and Author. She is a Master Embodiment Practitioner and Relationship and Sexuality Teacher and Coach. Dr. Kincaid is the Co-founder of The Institute of Integral Evolutionary Tantra and The Outrageous Love Project in New York City. She holds an M.A. and Doctorate in Theology. She is a graduate of the Institute of Core Energetics and the prestigious Barbara Brennan School of Healing, she also earned a B.A. in Anthropology from the University of Texas, Austin.

Kristina attributes her depth of insight and understanding of the body and the sexual to the profound wisdom teachings and transmissions given her over the years by her many incredible mentors and teachers as well as to her personal path of healing her own deep wounding around the sexual.

Kristina's passion is to teach conscious relating that is an affront to shame and guilt. Her commitment is to spark a movement with teachings and embodied practice that empower women and men to take responsibility for their own arousal and desire resulting in the full liberation and reclamation of their true potency and power.

Marc & Kristina have united to transform the desolate, raging landscape we have as a society, come to know as sex. Learn more about Kristina at DrKristinaKincaid.com.

kohlene hendrickson

...is a Fine Artist, Transformational Therapist and Creativity Coach.

She worked as an illustrator in Los Angeles for many years collaborating with such companies as Warner Bros and Geffen Records. Her male nude drawings were featured on the TV series Will & Grace and numerous artworks were used by set designers on television and film sets.

In parallel with her commercial work, she studied fresco painting with Frederico Vigil, a renowned fresco painter in the lineage of Diego Rivera. She continued her studies of fresco painting in Italy, where she discovered encaustic painting. Encaustic is an ancient painting technique which existed before the creation of oil paint. The historical Portraits of Fayum were painted with encaustics, which is a combination of natural materials, beeswax, damar resin and pigments. This polyvalent medium allows her to paint with transparency, movement and an unparalleled richness of material.

Moving to Switzerland in 2000, she immersed herself into fine arts and was represented by Plexus Art Gallery, one of the top galleries in Switzerland for many years. She continues to participate in international exhibitions and her art career has been recognized by distinguished awards.

– **Harmony for Humanity** –
The Global Consciousness Art Prize, 2023

– Contemporary Art Curator Magazine 2022,
The Faces of Peace Art Book

– **Primo Piano Atelier Prize** –
Silver Certificate Award *(Best technical execution),*
Curated exhibition in Lecce, Italy "Women's Solidarity" – Artwork "Shekhinah", 2020

– **International Artist of the Year** – *(female),*
by "Art Comes Alive 2019", ADC Fine Art, USA

– **Grant recipient awarded by the New York Council for the Arts** –
the "Inaugural Mario Venturini Artist Residency" at HAC FLX, 2015

– **Grand Prix Europeo Albrecht Dürer** –
the Accademia Gentilizia Il Marzocco of Florence for her painting "Awakening" in 2012

– **BoldBrush semi-finalist** –
for her painting "Double Vision"

The core inspiration of her artistic expression and life strongly resonates with the book *"**A Return To Eros**"*. Just a few pages into the book she felt she was reading what she had been painting all of her life. As she opened the book further, reading ***The Twelve Faces Of Eros***, it was clear she must paint them. The sacred Hebrew Tantric philosophy was an erotic mystical wisdom that needed to be painted and brought into the world. This is where the journey began. She's now a board member of the CIW, Center for Integral Wisdom and has found her unique voice as one who dances with and visually transmits EROS. Her artwork is both portal and invitation to the divine goddess "Shechinah. ***Eros*** as reality and ***"The Radical Experience Of Being Fully Alive"***.

"Kohlene's female figures in The Twelve Faces Of Eros manifest a sense of total well-being, peace, serenity, freedom, lightness, and a journey towards spiritual awakening, that place that embodies the hermeneutic criterion that crosses our time in the perspectives on human sexuality, on the love and the liberation of Eros" as written by Dores Sacquegna, Art Advisor & Curator of Contemporary Art, Lecce, Italy

Learn more about Kohlene's art and professional activities at

www.kohlene.com

www.kohlenehendrickson.com

Paintings and Drawings / originals and reproductions

To purchase original artworks contact the artist directly at **kohlene@kohlene.com**. Museum quality giclée prints are available, printed on Hahnemühle Torchon fine art paper. The prints are custom sized to fit the original artworks, the list below indicates the approximate size formats available with their respective prices.

Fine art print formats	***price***
70 x 100 cm / 27.5 x 39.5 inches	*$750*
50 x 70 cm / 19.5 x 27.5 inches	*$525*
21 x 28 cm / 8 x 11inches	*$75*

Series of the12 faces	***price***
21 x 28 cm / 8 x 11inches	*$750*

You may also order a custom size

An additional option to own an original artwork, the artist has developed a technique with an excellent result by printing museum quality giclée prints on Hahnemühle Torchon fine art paper, mounted on aluminum and hand finished by Kohlene with encaustic wax. The advantage is you can order a custom size to fit your space and the price is a portion of the original artwork. Contact the artist for more information.

www.ingramcontent.com/pod-product-compliance
Lightning Source LLC
LaVergne TN
LVHW070216110826
845147LV00003B/584